Environmental Issues

ENVIRONMENTAL POLICY

Environmental Issues

AIR QUALITY
CLIMATE CHANGE
CONSERVATION
ENVIRONMENTAL POLICY
WATER POLLUTION
WILDLIFE PROTECTION

Environmental Issues

ENVIRONMENTAL POLICY

Yael Calhoun
Series Editor

Foreword by David Seideman,
Editor-in-Chief, *Audubon* Magazine

CHELSEA HOUSE
PUBLISHERS
A Haights Cross Communications Company ®
Philadelphia

CHELSEA HOUSE PUBLISHERS

VP, NEW PRODUCT DEVELOPMENT Sally Cheney
DIRECTOR OF PRODUCTION Kim Shinners
CREATIVE MANAGER Takeshi Takahashi
MANUFACTURING MANAGER Diann Grasse

Staff for ENVIRONMENTAL POLICY

EXECUTIVE EDITOR Tara Koellhoffer
EDITORIAL ASSISTANT Kuorkor Dzani
PRODUCTION EDITOR Noelle Nardone
PHOTO EDITOR Sarah Bloom
SERIES AND COVER DESIGNER Keith Trego
LAYOUT 21st Century Publishing and Communications, Inc.

A Haights Cross Communications ✦ Company ®

First Printing

9 8 7 6 5 4 3 2 1

Library of Congress Cataloging-in-Publication Data

Environmental policy/[edited by Yael Calhoun]; foreword by
David Seideman.
    p. cm.—(Environmental issues)
        Includes bibliographical references and index.
    ISBN 0-7910-8205-9
    1. Environmental policy. I. Calhoun, Yael. II. Series.
GE170.E576683 2005
363.7'0561—dc22

                                                   2004028998

Contents Overview

Detailed Table of Contents

Foreword

by David Seideman, Editor-in-Chief, *Audubon* Magazine

For anyone contemplating the Earth's fate, there's probably no more instructive case study than the Florida Everglades. When European explorers first arrived there in the mid-1800s, they discovered a lush, tropical wilderness with dense sawgrass, marshes, mangrove forests, lakes, and tree islands. By the early 20th century, developers and politicians had begun building a series of canals and dikes to siphon off the region's water. They succeeded in creating an agricultural and real estate boom, and to some degree, they offset floods and droughts. But the ecological cost was exorbitant. Today, half of the Everglades' wetlands have been lost, its water is polluted by runoff from farms, and much of its wildlife, including Florida panthers and many wading birds such as wood storks, are hanging on by a thread.

Yet there has been a renewed sense of hope in the Everglades since 2001, when the state of Florida and the federal government approved a comprehensive $7.8 billion restoration plan, the biggest recovery of its kind in history. During the next four decades, ecologists and engineers will work to undo years of ecological damage by redirecting water back into the Everglades' dried-up marshes. "The Everglades are a test," says Joe Podger, an environmentalist. "If we pass, we get to keep the planet."

In fact, as this comprehensive series on environmental issues shows, humankind faces a host of tests that will determine whether we get to keep the planet. The world's crises—air and water pollution, the extinction of species, and climate change—are worsening by the day. The solutions—and there are many practical ones—all demand an extreme sense of urgency. E. O. Wilson, the noted Harvard zoologist, contends that "the world environment is changing so fast that there is a window of opportunity that will close in as little time as the next two or three decades." While Wilson's main concern is the rapid loss of biodiversity, he could have just as easily been discussing climate change or wetlands destruction.

The Earth is suffering the most massive extinction of species since the die-off of dinosaurs 65 million years ago. "If we continue at the current rate of deforestation and destruction of major ecosystems like rain forests and coral reefs, where most of the biodiversity is concentrated," Wilson says, "we will surely lose more than half of all the species of plants and animals on Earth by the end of the 21st century."

Many conservationists still mourn the loss of the passenger pigeon, which, as recently as the late 1800s, flew in miles-long flocks so dense they blocked the sun, turning noontime into nighttime. By 1914, target shooters and market hunters had reduced the species to a single individual, Martha, who lived at the Cincinnati Zoo until, as Peter Matthiessen wrote in *Wildlife in America,* "she blinked for the last time." Despite U.S. laws in place to avert other species from going the way of the passenger pigeon, the latest news is still alarming. In its 2004 State of the Birds report, Audubon noted that 70% of grassland bird species and 36% of shrubland bird species are suffering significant declines. Like the proverbial canary in the coalmine, birds serve as indicators, sounding the alarm about impending threats to environmental and human health.

Besides being an unmitigated moral tragedy, the disappearance of species has profound practical implications. Ninety percent of the world's food production now comes from about a dozen species of plants and eight species of livestock. Geneticists rely on wild populations to replenish varieties of domestic corn, wheat, and other crops, and to boost yields and resistance to disease. "Nature is a natural pharmacopoeia, and new drugs and medicines are being discovered in the wild all the time," wrote Niles Eldredge of the American Museum of Natural History, a noted author on the subject of extinction. "Aspirin comes from the bark of willow trees. Penicillin comes from a mold, a type of fungus." Furthermore, having a wide array of plants and animals improves a region's capacity to cleanse water, enrich soil, maintain stable climates, and produce the oxygen we breathe.

Today, the quality of the air we breathe and the water we drink does not augur well for our future health and well-being. Many people assume that the passage of the Clean Air Act in 1970 ushered in a new age. But the American Lung Association reports that 159 million Americans—55% of the population—are exposed to "unhealthy levels of air pollution." Meanwhile, the American Heart Association warns of a direct link between exposure to air pollution and heart disease and strokes. While it's true that U.S. waters are cleaner than they were three decades ago, data from the Environmental Protection Agency (EPA) shows that almost half of U.S. coastal waters fail to meet water-quality standards because they cannot support fishing or swimming. Each year, contaminated tap water makes as many as 7 million Americans sick. The chief cause is "non-point pollution," runoff that includes fertilizers and pesticides from farms and backyards as well as oil and chemical spills. On a global level, more than a billion people lack access to clean water; according to the United Nations, five times that number die each year from malaria and other illnesses associated with unsafe water.

Of all the Earth's critical environmental problems, one trumps the rest: climate change. Carol Browner, the EPA's chief from 1993 through 2001 (the longest term in the agency's history), calls climate change "the greatest environmental health problem the world has ever seen." Industry and people are spewing carbon dioxide from smokestacks and the tailpipes of their cars into the atmosphere, where a buildup of gases, acting like the glass in a greenhouse, traps the sun's heat. The 1990s was the warmest decade in more than a century, and 1998 saw the highest global temperatures ever. In an article about global climate change in the December 2003 issue of *Audubon*, David Malakoff wrote, "Among the possible consequences: rising sea levels that cause coastal communities to sink beneath the waves like a modern Atlantis, crop failures of biblical proportions, and once-rare killer storms that start to appear with alarming regularity."

Yet for all the doom and gloom, scientists and environmentalists hold out hope. When Russia recently ratified the Kyoto Protocol, it meant that virtually all of the world's industrialized nations—the United States, which has refused to sign, is a notable exception—have committed to cutting greenhouse gases. As Kyoto and other international agreements go into effect, a market is developing for cap-and-trade systems for carbon dioxide. In this country, two dozen big corporations, including British Petroleum, are cutting emissions. At least 28 American states have adopted their own policies. California, for example, has passed global warming legislation aimed at curbing emissions from new cars. Governor Arnold Schwarzenegger has also backed regulations requiring automakers to slash the amount of greenhouse gases they cause by up to 30% by 2016, setting a precedent for other states.

As Washington pushes a business-friendly agenda, states are filling in the policy vacuum in other areas, as well. California and New York are developing laws to preserve wetlands, which filter pollutants, prevent floods, and provide habitat for endangered wildlife.

By taking matters into their own hands, states and foreign countries will ultimately force Washington's. What industry especially abhors is a crazy quilt of varying rules. After all, it makes little sense for a company to invest a billion dollars in a power plant only to find out later that it has to spend even more to comply with another state's stricter emissions standards. Ford chairman and chief executive William Ford has lashed out at the states' "patchwork" approach because he and "other manufacturers will have a hard time responding." Further, he wrote in a letter to his company's top managers, "the prospect of 50 different requirements in 50 different states would be nothing short of chaos." The type of fears Ford expresses are precisely the reason federal laws protecting clean air and water came into being.

Governments must take the lead, but ecologically conscious consumers wield enormous influence, too. Over the past four decades, the annual use of pesticides has more than doubled, from 215 million pounds to 511 million pounds. Each year, these poisons cause $10 billion worth of damage to the environment and kill 72 million birds. The good news is that the demand for organic products is revolutionizing agriculture, in part by creating a market for natural alternatives for pest control. Some industry experts predict that by 2007 the organic industry will almost quadruple, to more than $30 billion.

E. O. Wilson touts "shade-grown" coffee as one of many "personal habitats that, if moderated only in this country, could contribute significantly to saving endangered species." In the mountains of Mexico and Central America, coffee grown beneath a dense forest canopy rather than in cleared fields helps provide refuge for dozens of wintering North American migratory bird species, from western tanagers to Baltimore orioles.

With conservation such a huge part of Americans' daily routine, recycling has become as ingrained a civic duty as obeying traffic lights. Californians, for their part, have cut their energy consumption by 10% each year since the state's 2001 energy crisis. "Poll after poll shows that about two-thirds of the American public—Democrat and Republican, urban and rural—consider environmental progress crucial," writes Carl Pope, director of the Sierra Club, in his recent book, *Strategic Ignorance*. "Clean air, clean water, wilderness preservation— these are such bedrock values that many polling respondents find it hard to believe that any politician would oppose them."

Terrorism and the economy clearly dwarfed all other issues in the 2004 presidential election. Even so, voters approved 120 out of 161 state and local conservation funding measures nationwide, worth a total of $3.25 billion. Anti-environment votes in the U.S. Congress and proposals floated by the like-minded Bush administration should not obscure the salient fact that so far there have been no changes to the major environmental laws. The potential for political fallout is too great.

The United States' legacy of preserving its natural heritage is the envy of the world. Our national park system alone draws more than 300 million visitors each year. Less well known is the 103-year-old national wildlife refuge system you'll learn about in this series. Its unique mission is to safeguard the nation's wild animals and plants on 540 refuges, protecting 700 species of birds and an equal number of other vertebrates; 282 of these species are either threatened or endangered. One of the many species particularly dependent on the invaluable habitat refuges afford is the bald eagle. Such safe havens, combined with the banning of the insecticide DDT and enforcement of the

Endangered Species Act, have led to the bald eagle's remarkable recovery, from a low of 500 breeding pairs in 1963 to 7,600 today. In fact, this bird, the national symbol of the United States, is about be removed from the endangered species list and downgraded to a less threatened status under the CITES, the Convention on International Trade in Endangered Species.

This vital treaty, upheld by the United States and 165 other participating nations (and detailed in this series), underscores the worldwide will to safeguard much of the Earth's magnificent wildlife. Since going into effect in 1975, CITES has helped enact plans to save tigers, chimpanzees, and African elephants. These species and many others continue to face dire threats from everything from poaching to deforestation. At the same time, political progress is still being made. Organizations like the World Wildlife Fund work tirelessly to save these species from extinction because so many millions of people care. China, for example, the most populous nation on Earth, is so concerned about its giant pandas that it has implemented an ambitious captive breeding program. That program's success, along with government measures prohibiting logging throughout the panda's range, may actually enable the remaining population of 1,600 pandas to hold its own—and perhaps grow. "For the People's Republic of China, pressure intensified as its internationally popular icon edged closer to extinction," wrote Gerry Ellis in a recent issue of *National Wildlife.* "The giant panda was not only a poster child for endangered species, it was a symbol of our willingness to ensure nature's place on Earth."

Whether people take a spiritual path to conservation or a pragmatic one, they ultimately arrive at the same destination. The sight of a bald eagle soaring across the horizon reassures us about nature's resilience, even as the clean air and water we both need to survive becomes less of a certainty. "The conservation of our natural resources and their proper use constitute the fundamental problem which underlies almost every other problem of our national life," President Theodore Roosevelt told Congress at the dawn of the conservation movement a century ago. His words ring truer today than ever.

Introduction: "Why Should We Care?"

Our nation's air and water are cleaner today than they were 30 years ago. After a century of filling and destroying over half of our wetlands, we now protect many of them. But the Earth is getting warmer, habitats are being lost to development and logging, and humans are using more water than ever before. Increased use of water can leave rivers, lakes, and wetlands without enough water to support the native plant and animal life. Such changes are causing plants and animals to go extinct at an increased rate. It is no longer a question of losing just the dodo birds or the passenger pigeons, argues David Quammen, author of *Song of the Dodo*: "Within a few decades, if present trends continue, we'll be losing *a lot* of everything." [1]

In the 1980s, E. O. Wilson, a Harvard biologist and Pulitzer Prize–winning author, helped bring the term *biodiversity* into public discussions about conservation. *Biodiversity*, short for "biological diversity," refers to the levels of organization for living things. Living organisms are divided and categorized into ecosystems (such as rain forests or oceans), by species (such as mountain gorillas), and by genetics (the genes responsible for inherited traits).

Wilson has predicted that if we continue to destroy habitats and pollute the Earth at the current rate, in 50 years, we could lose 30 to 50% of the planet's species to extinction. In his 1992 book, *The Diversity of Life*, Wilson asks: "Why should we care?" [2] His long list of answers to this question includes: the potential loss of vast amounts of scientific information that would enable the development of new crops, products, and medicines and the potential loss of the vast economic and environmental benefits of healthy ecosystems. He argues that since we have only a vague idea (even with our advanced scientific methods) of how ecosystems really work, it would be "reckless" to suppose that destroying species indefinitely will not threaten us all in ways we may not even understand.

THE BOOKS IN THE SERIES

In looking at environmental issues, it quickly becomes clear that, as naturalist John Muir once said, "When we try to pick out anything by itself, we find it hitched to everything else in the Universe."[3] For example, air pollution in one state or in one country can affect not only air quality in another place, but also land and water quality. Soil particles from degraded African lands can blow across the ocean and cause damage to far-off coral reefs.

The six books in this series address a variety of environmental issues: conservation, wildlife protection, water pollution, air quality, climate change, and environmental policy. None of these can be viewed as a separate issue. Air quality impacts climate change, wildlife, and water quality. Conservation initiatives directly affect water and air quality, climate change, and wildlife protection. Endangered species are touched by each of these issues. And finally, environmental policy issues serve as important tools in addressing all the other environmental problems that face us.

You can use the burning of coal as an example to look at how a single activity directly "hitches" to a variety of environmental issues. Humans have been burning coal as a fuel for hundreds of years. The mining of coal can leave the land stripped of vegetation, which erodes the soil. Soil erosion contributes to particulates in the air and water quality problems. Mining coal can also leave piles of acidic tailings that degrade habitats and pollute water. Burning any fossil fuel—coal, gas, or oil—releases large amounts of carbon dioxide into the atmosphere. Carbon dioxide is considered a major "greenhouse gas" that contributes to global warming—the gradual increase in the Earth's temperature over time. In addition, coal burning adds sulfur dioxide to the air, which contributes to the formation of acid rain—precipitation that is abnormally acidic. This acid rain can kill forests and leave lakes too acidic to support life. Technology continues to present ways to minimize the pollution that results from extracting and burning fossil fuels. Clean air and climate change policies guide states and industries toward implementing various strategies and technologies for a cleaner coal industry.

Each of the six books in this series—ENVIRONMENTAL ISSUES—introduces the significant points that relate to the specific topic and explains its relationship to other environmental concerns.

Book One: *Air Quality*

Problems of air pollution can be traced back to the time when humans first started to burn coal. *Air Quality* looks at today's challenges in fighting to keep our air clean and safe. The book includes discussions of air pollution sources—car and truck emissions, diesel engines, and many industries. It also discusses their effects on our health and the environment.

The Environmental Protection Agency (EPA) has reported that more than 150 million Americans live in areas that have unhealthy levels of some type of air pollution.[4] Today, more than 20 million Americans, over 6 million of whom are children, suffer from asthma believed to be triggered by pollutants in the air.[5]

In 1970, Congress passed the Clean Air Act, putting in place an ambitious set of regulations to address air pollution concerns. The EPA has identified and set standards for six common air pollutants: ground-level ozone, nitrogen oxides, particulate matter, sulfur dioxide, carbon monoxide, and lead.

The EPA has also been developing the Clean Air Rules of 2004, national standards aimed at improving the country's air quality by specifically addressing the many sources of contaminants. However, many conservation organizations and even some states have concerns over what appears to be an attempt to weaken different sections of the 1990 version of the Clean Air Act. The government's environmental protection efforts take on increasing importance because air pollution degrades land and water, contributes to global warming, and affects the health of plants and animals, including humans.

Book Two: *Climate Change*

Part of science is observing patterns, and scientists have observed a global rise in temperature. *Climate Change* discusses the sources and effects of global warming. Scientists attribute this accelerated change to human activities such as the burning of fossil fuels that emit greenhouse gases (GHG).[6] Since the 1700s, we have been cutting down the trees that help remove carbon dioxide from the atmosphere, and have increased the amount of coal, gas, and oil we burn, all of which add carbon dioxide to the atmosphere. Science tells us that these human activities have caused greenhouse gases—carbon dioxide (CO_2), methane (CH_4), nitrous oxide (N_2O), hydrofluorocarbons (HFCs), perfluorocarbons (PFCs), and sulfur hexafluoride (SF_6)—to accumulate in the atmosphere.[7]

If the warming patterns continue, scientists warn of more negative environmental changes. The effects of climate change, or global warming, can be seen all over the world. Thousands of scientists are predicting rising sea levels, disturbances in patterns of rainfall and regional weather, and changes in ranges and reproductive cycles of plants and animals. Climate change is already having some effects on certain plant and animal species.[8]

Many countries and some American states are already working together and with industries to reduce the emissions of greenhouse gases. Climate change is an issue that clearly fits noted scientist Rene Dubois's advice: "Think globally, act locally."

Book Three: *Conservation*

Conservation considers the issues that affect our world's vast array of living creatures and the land, water, and air they need to survive.

One of the first people in the United States to put the political spotlight on conservation ideas was President Theodore Roosevelt. In the early 1900s, he formulated policies and created programs that addressed his belief that: "The nation behaves well if it treats the natural resources as assets which it must turn over to the next generation increased, and not impaired, in value."[9] In the 1960s, biologist Rachel Carson's book, *Silent Spring*, brought conservation issues into the public eye. People began to see that polluted land, water, and air affected their health. The 1970s brought the creation of the United States Environmental Protection Agency (EPA) and passage of many federal and state rules and regulations to protect the quality of our environment and our health.

Some 80 years after Theodore Roosevelt established the first National Wildlife Refuge in 1903, Harvard biologist

E. O. Wilson brought public awareness of conservation issues to a new level. He warned:

> . . . the worst thing that will probably happen—in fact is already well underway—is not energy depletion, economic collapse, conventional war, or even the expansion of totalitarian governments. As terrible as these catastrophes would be for us, they can be repaired within a few generations. The one process now ongoing that will take million of years to correct is the loss of genetic species diversity by the destruction of natural habitats. This is the folly our descendants are least likely to forgive us.[10]

To heed Wilson's warning means we must strive to protect species-rich habitats, or "hotspots," such as tropical rain forests and coral reefs. It means dealing with conservation concerns like soil erosion and pollution of fresh water and of the oceans. It means protecting sea and land habitats from the over-exploitation of resources. And it means getting people involved on all levels—from national and international government agencies, to private conservation organizations, to the individual person who recycles or volunteers to listen for the sounds of frogs in the spring.

Book Four: *Environmental Policy*

One approach to solving environmental problems is to develop regulations and standards of safety. Just as there are rules for living in a community or for driving on a road, there are environmental regulations and policies that work toward protecting our health and our lands. *Environmental Policy* discusses the regulations and programs that have been crafted to address environmental issues at all levels—global, national, state, and local.

Today, as our resources become increasingly limited, we witness heated debates about how to use our public lands and how to protect the quality of our air and water. Should we allow drilling in the Arctic National Wildlife Refuge? Should we protect more marine areas? Should we more closely regulate the emissions of vehicles, ships, and industries? These policy issues, and many more, continue to make news on a daily basis.

In addition, environmental policy has taken a place on the international front. Hundreds of countries are working together in a variety of ways to address such issues as global warming, air pollution, water pollution and supply, land preservation, and the protection of endangered species. One question the United States continues to debate is whether to sign the 1997 Kyoto Protocol, the international agreement designed to decrease the emissions of greenhouse gases.

Many of the policy tools for protecting our environment are already in place. It remains a question how they will be used—and whether they will be put into action in time to save our natural resources and ourselves.

Book Five: *Water Pollution*

Pollution can affect water everywhere. Pollution in lakes and rivers is easily seen. But water that is out of our plain view can also be polluted with substances such as toxic chemicals, fertilizers, pesticides, oils, and gasoline. *Water Pollution* considers issues of concern to our surface waters, our groundwater, and our oceans.

In the early 1970s, about three-quarters of the water in the United States was considered unsafe for swimming and fishing. When Lake Erie was declared "dead" from pollution and a river feeding it actually caught on fire, people decided that the national government had to take a stronger role in protecting our resources. In 1972, Congress passed the Clean Water Act, a law whose objective "is to restore and maintain the chemical, physical, and biological integrity of the Nation's waters."[11] Today, over 30 years later, many lakes and rivers have been restored to health. Still, an estimated 40% of our waters are still unsafe to swim in or fish.

Less than 1% of the available water on the planet is fresh water. As the world's population grows, our demand for drinking and irrigation water increases. Therefore, the quantity of available water has become a major global issue. As Sandra Postel, a leading authority on international freshwater issues, says, "Water scarcity is now the single biggest threat to global food production."[12] Because there are many competing demands for water, including the needs of habitats, water pollution continues to become an even more serious problem each year.

Book Six: *Wildlife Protection*

For many years, the word *wildlife* meant only the animals that people hunted for food or for sport. It was not until 1986 that the Oxford English Dictionary defined *wildlife* as "the native fauna and flora of a particular region."[13] *Wildlife Protection* looks at overexploitation—for example, overfishing or collecting plants and animals for illegal trade—and habitat loss. Habitat loss can be the result of development, logging, pollution, water diverted for human use, air pollution, and climate change.

Also discussed are various approaches to wildlife protection. Since protection of wildlife is an issue of global concern, it is addressed here on international as well as on national and local levels. Topics include voluntary international organizations such as the International Whaling Commission and the CITES agreements on trade in endangered species. In the United States, the Endangered Species Act provides legal protection for more than 1,200 different plant and animal species. Another approach to wildlife protection includes developing partnerships among conservation organizations, governments, and local people to foster economic incentives to protect wildlife.

CONSERVATION IN THE UNITED STATES

Those who first lived on this land, the Native American peoples, believed in general that land was held in common, not to be individually owned, fenced, or tamed. The white settlers from Europe had very different views of land. Some believed the New World was a Garden of Eden. It was a land of opportunity for them, but it was also a land to be controlled and subdued. Ideas on how to treat the land often followed those of European thinkers like John Locke, who believed that "Land that is left wholly to nature is called, as indeed it is, waste." [14]

The 1800s brought another way of approaching the land. Thinkers such as Ralph Waldo Emerson, John Muir, and Henry David Thoreau celebrated our human connection with nature. By the end of the 1800s, some scientists and policymakers were noticing the damage humans have caused to the land. Leading public officials preached stewardship and wise use of our country's resources. In 1873, Yellowstone National Park was set up. In 1903, the first National Wildlife Refuge was established.

However, most of the government practices until the middle of the 20th century favored unregulated development and use of the land's resources. Forests were clear cut, rivers were dammed, wetlands were filled to create farmland, and factories were allowed to dump their untreated waste into rivers and lakes.

In 1949, a forester and ecologist named Aldo Leopold revived the concept of preserving land for its own sake. But there was now a biological, or scientific, reason for conservation, not just a spiritual one. Leopold declared: "All ethics rest upon a single premise: that the individual is a member of a community of interdependent parts. . . . A thing is right when it tends to preserve the integrity and stability and beauty of the biotic community. It is wrong when it tends otherwise." [15]

The fiery vision of these conservationists helped shape a more far-reaching movement that began in the 1960s. Many credit Rachel Carson's eloquent and accessible writings, such as her 1962 book *Silent Spring*, with bringing environmental issues into people's everyday language. When the Cuyahoga River in Ohio caught fire in 1969 because it was so polluted, it captured the public attention. Conservation was no longer just about protecting land that many people would never even see, it was about protecting human health. The condition of the environment had become personal.

In response to the public outcry about water and air pollution, the 1970s saw the establishment of the EPA. Important legislation to protect the air and water was passed. National standards for a cleaner environment were set and programs were established to help achieve the ambitious goals. Conservation organizations grew from what had started as exclusive white men's hunting clubs to interest groups with a broad membership base. People came together to demand changes that would afford more protection to the environment and to their health.

Since the 1960s, some presidential administrations have sought to strengthen environmental protection and to protect more land and national treasures. For example, in 1980, President Jimmy Carter signed an act that doubled the amount of protected land in Alaska and renamed it the Arctic National Wildlife Refuge. Other administrations, like those of President Ronald Reagan, sought to dismantle many earlier environmental protection initiatives.

The environmental movement, or environmentalism, is not one single, homogeneous cause. The agencies, individuals, and organizations that work toward protecting the environment vary as widely as the habitats and places they seek to protect. There are individuals who begin grass-roots efforts—people like Lois Marie Gibbs, a former resident of the polluted area of Love Canal, New York, who founded the Center for Health, Environment and Justice. There are conservation organizations, like The Nature Conservancy, the World Wildlife Fund (WWF), and Conservation International, that sponsor programs to preserve and protect habitats. There are groups that specialize in monitoring public policy and legislation—for example, the Natural Resources Defense Council and Environmental Defense. In addition, there are organizations like the Audubon Society and the National Wildlife Federation whose focus is on public education about environmental issues. Perhaps from this diversity, just like there exists in a healthy ecosystem, will come the strength and vision environmentalism needs to deal with the continuing issues of the 21st century.

INTERNATIONAL CONSERVATION EFFORTS

In his book *Biodiversity*, E. O. Wilson cautions that biological diversity must be taken seriously as a global resource for three reasons. First, human population growth is accelerating the degrading of the environment, especially in tropical countries. Second, science continues to discover new uses for biological diversity—uses that can benefit human health and protect the environment. And third, much biodiversity is being lost through extinction, much of it in the tropics. As Wilson states, "We must hurry to acquire the knowledge on which a wise policy of conservation and development can be based for centuries to come."[16]

People organize themselves within boundaries and borders. But oceans, rivers, air, and wildlife do not follow such rules. Pollution or overfishing in one part of an ocean can easily degrade the quality of another country's resources. If one country diverts a river, it can destroy another country's wetlands or water resources. When Wilson cautions us that we must hurry to develop a wise conservation policy, he means a policy that will protect resources all over the world.

To accomplish this will require countries to work together on critical global issues: preserving biodiversity, reducing global warming, decreasing air pollution, and protecting the oceans. There are many important international efforts already going on to protect the resources of our planet. Some efforts are regulatory, while others are being pursued by nongovernmental organizations or private conservation groups.

Countries volunteering to cooperate to protect resources is not a new idea. In 1946, a group of countries established the International Whaling Commission (IWC). They recognized that unregulated whaling around the world had led to severe declines in the world's whale populations. In 1986, the IWC declared a moratorium on whaling, which is still in effect, until the populations have recovered.[17] Another example of international cooperation occurred in 1987 when various countries signed the Montreal Protocol to reduce the emissions of ozone-depleting gases. It has been a huge success, and perhaps has served as a model for other international efforts, like the 1997 Kyoto Protocol, to limit emissions of greenhouse gases.

Yet another example of international environmental cooperation is the CITES agreement (the Convention on International Trade in Endangered Species of Wild Fauna and Flora), a legally binding agreement to ensure that the international trade of plants and animals does not threaten the species' survival. CITES went into force in 1975 after 80 countries agreed to the terms. Today, it has grown to include more than 160 countries. This make CITES among the largest conservation agreements in existence.[18]

Another show of international conservation efforts are governments developing economic incentives for local conservation. For example, in 1996, the International Monetary Fund (IMF) and the World Wildlife Fund (WWF) established a program to relieve poor countries of debt. More than 40 countries have benefited by agreeing to direct some of their savings toward environmental programs in the "Debt-for-Nature" swap programs.[19]

It is worth our time to consider the thoughts of two American conservationists and what role we, as individuals, can play in conserving and protecting our world. E. O. Wilson has told us that "Biological Diversity—'biodiversity' in the new parlance—is the key to the maintenance of the world as we know it."[20] Aldo Leopold, the forester who gave Americans the idea of creating a "land ethic," wrote in 1949 that: "Having to squeeze the last drop of utility out of the land has the same desperate finality as having to chop up the furniture to keep warm."[21] All of us have the ability to take part in the struggle to protect our environment and to save our endangered Earth.

ENDNOTES

1   Quammen, David. *Song of the Dodo.* New York: Scribner, 1996, p. 607.

2   Wilson, E. O. *Diversity of Life.* Cambridge, MA: Harvard University Press, 1992, p. 346.

3   Muir, John. *My First Summer in the Sierra.* San Francisco: Sierra Club Books, 1988, p. 110.

4 Press Release. *EPA Newsroom: EPA Issues Designations on Ozone Health Standards.* April 15, 2004. Available online at *http://www.epa.gov/newsroom/.*

5 The Environmental Protection Agency. EPA Newsroom. *May is Allergy Awareness Month.* May 2004. Available online at *http://www.epa.gov/newsroom/allergy_month.htm.*

6 Intergovernmental Panel on Climate Change (IPCC). Third Annual Report, 2001.

7 Turco, Richard P. *Earth Under Siege: From Air Pollution to Global Change.* New York: Oxford University Press, 2002, p. 387.

8 Intergovernmental Panel on Climate Change. *Technical Report V: Climate Change and Biodiversity.* 2002. Full report available online at *http://www.ipcc.ch/pub/tpbiodiv.pdf.*

9 "Roosevelt Quotes." American Museum of Natural History. Available online at *http://www.amnh.org/common/faq/quotes.html.*

10 Wilson, E. O. *Biophilia.* Cambridge, MA: Harvard University Press, 1986, pp. 10–11.

11 Federal Water Pollution Control Act. As amended November 27, 2002. Section 101 (a).

12 Postel, Sandra. *Pillars of Sand.* New York: W. W. Norton & Company, Inc., 1999. p. 6.

13 Hunter, Malcolm L. *Wildlife, Forests, and Forestry: Principles of Managing Forest for Biological Diversity.* Englewood Cliffs, NJ: Prentice-Hall, 1990, p. 4.

14 Dowie, Mark. *Losing Ground: American Environmentalism at the Close of the Twentieth Century.* Cambridge, MA: MIT Press, 1995, p. 113.

15 Leopold, Aldo. *A Sand County Almanac.* New York: Oxford University Press, 1949.

16 Wilson, E. O., ed. *Biodiversity.* Washington, D.C.: National Academies Press, 1988, p. 3.

17 International Whaling Commission Information 2004. Available online at *http://www.iwcoffice.org/commission/iwcmain.htm.*

18 *Discover CITES: What is CITES?* Fact sheet 2004. Available online at *http://www.cites.org/eng/disc/what.shtml.*

19 *Madagascar's Experience with Swapping Debt for the Environment.* World Wildlife Fund Report, 2003. Available online at *http://www.conservationfinance.org/WPC/WPC_documents/Apps_11_Moye_Paddack_v2.pdf.*

20 Wilson, *Diversity of Life,* p. 15.

21 Leopold.

What Are Public Lands and Who Decides How They Are Used?

The founding democratic ideals of the United States rested on people's ability to own land. The American Revolution ensured that the European practice of kings claiming the land's resources would not happen here. Today, Americans as a group own about 740 million acres of public land, nearly one-third of the country's total mass. These lands are federal lands—national parks, wildlife refuges, forests, marine sanctuaries, and historic monuments. In his book *This Is Your Land: The Struggle to Save America's Public Lands*, Bernard Shanks outlines U.S. public land issues.

The competing public land goals of careful resource management versus resource extraction has resulted in a growing conflict. Time and economic studies have shown that recreational use of undeveloped public lands brings the nation billions of dollars in economic benefits.[1] Public lands also protect wilderness, endangered species, and cultural landmarks. In 1903, President Theodore Roosevelt put the ideas of conservation into public policy by starting the National Wildlife Refuge program. His goal was to strike a balance between using resources now and keeping the land healthy for future generations to enjoy.

On the other hand, old mining laws and grazing regulations have traditionally allowed only a few people to benefit from the land that belongs to us all. In addition, some government administrations have supported policies that open up more and more public lands to oil and gas drilling. Today, the debate over gas and oil drilling on public lands is being played out in the Rocky Mountain states and in the Arctic National Wildlife Refuge. The struggle also continues in federal proposals to put roads through national forests to increase the timber harvest. Water pollution, air pollution, and funding for public lands management are other related issues.

Although Shanks's book was published over 20 years ago, the issues that he identified have grown even more relevant with time. Science has given us knowledge about the importance of wise resource management. Now we must decide, through the democratic process, how to apply that knowledge to both present use and future preservation of federal lands.

—The Editor

1. Natural Resources Defense Council. "Why We Need Public Lands." Factsheet. Available online at *http://www.nrdc.org/land/use/fplval.asp*.

The Heart of the Nation
by Bernard Shanks

As a nation we own lands whose beauty seizes the heart. As Americans, we can stand on our own land at the rim of the Grand Canyon and look into a winter storm, or walk among the geysers of Yellowstone and share the land with grazing elk and bison. On a spring night, with the moon lighting Yosemite Valley, we can listen to the power of a Sierra winter melting.

The allure of the open lands the public owns is a haunting dream, from Assateague Island to the western prow of Point Reyes. Their magic and primal freedom are found along the Yukon River, embodied in a wolf track. Their essence is in the elegant song of a cactus wren as the sun rises over the Sonoran Desert. The people of our nation own the Great Plains, with their smell of short prairie grass after a summer thunderstorm and their fluid music of meadowlarks lifting the eyes and heart to a promising horizon. Beauty is everywhere on the people's lands: in the cool relief of shadows that slide out of the mountains when the sun drops across Nevada's Black Rock Desert; in the labyrinthian redrock canyons of the Colorado Plateau; in the resonant heat of Oregon's stark basalt plains; under a humid blanket of air in the Everglades. The publicly owned lands are the ideal lands of America, the pristine continent from which the nation rose to greatness.

We own them as a people, and the federal government manages them. They are the spiritual heart of this nation, and because of the forces of history and geography, they are also the most evocative territories in the country. The public lands are extremes: the highest peaks, the lowest deserts, the wildest and most exotic regions. They hold relics of the stone age, the spirit of the frontier, and the enchantment found only in the earth's wild heart. They are the most substantial measure of the nation's wealth and an essential source of individual freedom, power, and renewal. They are the most tangible resources for our future generations. Protecting them is a sacred public trust so this generation can provide an endowment to the future.

Public lands are fascinating because they remain largely untamed and primeval. These lands, in a world of asphalt and urbanization, are remnants of a nation once completely wild. They contrast with the attractions of the modern world, in which nature's subtly elegant beauty is shown on a billboard behind some artificial product whose value is measured by its ability to arrest attention. Each area of public lands is distinctive and without comparison; none of them can be replaced by private lands any more than a rainbow can be replaced by McDonald's arches.

Lands used in common by a people were part of the earliest civilizations—Greek, Roman, African, and Asian. Native Americans regarded land not merely as community property, but as elemental wealth held by community tenure. Land was so critical to life that no single generation could be trusted with ownership. Not only American Indians, but people throughout the world who had a direct tie to the earth and its resources considered hunting grounds, grazing regions, and upland watersheds to be held by the community as a trust. The European concept of land as property was totally alien to the Indians. When the Native Americans lost their tribal common lands, they suffered a cultural earthquake that shattered their world.

More than 200 years ago the glint of wildland helped fire the American Revolution. Land was not only a focus of the war, but a weapon to win and a prize for the victors. Revolution won the United States a vast domain, a source of wealth, power, and freedom without equal in the world. When the royal decrees were nullified, the land belonged to the new American nation. Federal land provided the freedom to choose a national goal, the power for manifest destiny, and the wealth to pay the price. It provided cash for Jefferson's great bargain with the French, expanding national boundaries westward with the Louisiana Purchase. It was the raw material that built America.

Public land that could be claimed was a beacon drawing settlers West. It pulled miners to California, farmers to Oregon, loggers to the forests, and ranchers to the plains. The Marines marched into Mexico City to seize that country's northern territory; land was the essence of manifest destiny. The drive to enlarge the national territory and the individual freedom to claim and settle it dominated Congress for a hundred years.

Then, with the collapse of the frontier, public lands came to mean more than capital. The country realized that a vital force in American democracy would be missed. Not only the frontier, but the hope of land for every citizen was coming to an end; with it would end a source of strength in the national life and an important crucible for democracy. At the time Frederick Jackson Turner explained the loss of the frontier, Theodore Roosevelt was driving home the essential truth that a nation was only as strong as its resources. Wasting and destroying natural resources weaken a nation as surely as the ravages of war. Protecting public resources came to be seen as not only essential ecologically, but an act of patriotism.

At the beginning of the twentieth century, a major national social reform—conservation—became the guiding ethic for federal lands. Several historic forces came together at once: geographic limits of the land had been reached; population had grown; and social change forced a new but imperfect system of federal land management. At its core was conservation. Conservation was intended to provide a multitude of public values and benefits and to be democratically applied. But many opportunities remained for private plunder. The science of conservation, the requirement for national security, and the obligations to future generations could not defeat the drive for private profit.

Congressional debate reflected fundamental national rifts concerning the public lands. The conflicts were between aristocratic and democratic philosophies of government, and a corporate and common-citizen approach to economics, always amid regional tensions. The landed opposed the landless. The West battled the East. After World War II the hundred-year regional polarization shifted to an urban-versus-rural conflict. Sharp differences of opinion have persisted in how to time the development of land and resources. Planning has often been argued in terms of preservation versus development, but more accurately the debate reflected a contest between using resources today or conserving them for future generations. Throughout congressional and other political debate, the importance of our common lands in our current national life has been ignored.

Public lands are far more than territory. They are an artifact of history, a source of beauty, inspiration, and greed. They are a durable standard of public wealth, a source of both economic and personal power. Public lands are part of our national heritage. The finest national gifts we have received and can give to the future are parks, wildlife refuges, and wild rivers. In contrast, the darkest tales of nineteenth-century American development were woven around the waste, destruction, and theft of public land and resources.

Seeing the land provides a perspective on the history and the spiritual geography of our nation. Rusting fragments of pioneer wagons still sit beside the ruts of trails. The long route the pony express pounded still traces a path from mountain pass to desert spring and over the next pass. Camping beside it in the Great Basin raises an apparition of a small, tough man riding out of the past with a pounding of hooves and the slap of leather. Old forts molder in the sun. National parks and monuments recreate historic scenes from Gettysburg to the Little Big Horn, from the Everglades swamps to the dry hostility of Death Valley.

Thousands of remote western canyons hold messages of an even earlier age, left when hunters and warriors etched petroglyphs in the rocks. In the canyons of Utah an ancient grain-storage bin with dry corn cobs lets anyone grasp more personal lessons of human survival than any in a museum display. A broken arrowhead by a desert spring tells volumes about the skill and life of an earlier warrior. In a world plagued by nuclear warriors, a broad historical perspective on life, survival, and the role of human species on the earth is rare. When found, it is to be cherished.

America's federal lands are one place to find the diversity of the natural world on a large scale, in contrast to the regimentation of a cornfield or the monotony of mile upon mile of wheat. On federal lands big, unconfined wild creatures roam, and humans see them naturally from a distance, not domestically confined behind a concrete moat or bars. The passion of a wild peregrine falcon's cry cannot be duplicated by urban pigeons cooing on courthouse eaves. Public lands provide fleeting glimpses of a rangy coyote, not a manicured poodle on a leash. These lands have the elegance of wild nature, and they inspire visions and dreams, not just profits and products. They are beautiful because they are wild, open, and free.

One of the greatest benefits public lands provide individuals is physical freedom. In a world ever more crowded and confined, the freedom to roam over big mountains and wide valleys is priceless. Private land often becomes a personal fortress for people threatened by crime, crowds, and urban pressures. It is often closed in. On public lands the open space and human freedom that guided a national destiny and shaped a democratic heritage can still be experienced.

It is in this freedom that American people find their personal share of the public wealth. Using public lands for hiking, sightseeing, and spiritual re-creation is a democratic activity millions of people enjoy every year. Unlike economic development, outdoor activities are not commercial practices. They are the physical and psychological benefits earned by virtue of American citizenship.

The wealth of our lands takes many economic forms, too, however. The people own 740 million acres of land, nearly one-third of the entire nation. The lands also include more than a billion acres of outer-continental shelf, which contains most oil and gas reserves—more than 36 billion barrels of oil and 178 trillion cubic feet of gas. At today's prices, those publicly-owned resources are worth more than $1.3 trillion and are appreciating each year. The nationally-owned coal, oil shale, and other energy resources are worth trillions more. Between 97 and 98 percent of the silver known in the nation comes from land currently or formerly public. Large copper, zinc, gold, and other deposits are under the public domain.

Despite their wealth, however, these mineral lands earn the owners, the American public, no royalties and little rent. Long ago mining and energy companies learned how to gain title to the public minerals, mine the land, and leave the public with a dry husk.

Another source of wealth on the public lands is the grass, the basis of life for native wild animals, wild horses, domestic sheep, goats, and cattle. But its unequal distribution among species tells the problem: most of the grass and forage is claimed by stock raisers at below-market prices to feed domestic livestock, leaving about 10 percent for native wildlife and wild horses. Because of a long history of overgrazing, grass and forage are depleted and soils are eroding. Domestic animals' grazing on public lands in the West is the single most important factor in American desertification. The cattle raised there supply us with only 3 percent of our beef.

Because of the geography of western land, most rain and snow falls on public land. But economics and tradition insist that water, the most precious of western resources, be captured for the profit of private corporations. Not only is the water transferred to private hands, expensive dams and delivery systems are largely paid for by taxpayers. Public lands capture the water, but after thousands of sluices channel it to private hands, only a trickle is left for the people.

There is a conflict between the public that owns the lands and the businesses that capture the resources. Many developers see not the beauty of the land, but the bottom line of a corporate ledger. Others see land in tidy philosophical adages, applying free-market theory and trickle-down economics. Still others see land in political terms as a battleground between environmentalists and business people. The people and corporations who use the lands have always demanded control, but private profit cannot be a substitute for public trust. Public land must have a unique standard of management, a land ethic distinct from private property.

The miner does not see a fragile surface layer of soil, grass, flowers, and herbs, but rather the rock outcrop that hints of secret lodes below—then breaks away the pioneer of lichen, the better to read a story of crystals, minerals, and gold. Land broken and shattered by thousands of earthquakes and countless storms is not a source of a miner's wonder and mystery, and fractured rock, a measure of the earth's inner torments or the invisible strength of frost, is not a riddle. The miracle called soil, the mystical soup of long-dead leaves, grass, flowers, insects, minerals, and moisture is a priceless resource; but it is overburden to the miner, a worthless product hiding El Dorado.

To the cattle ranchers, larkspur is an enemy, not a colorful reminder of a summer day to be pressed into a guidebook. To the stock raisers, the mix of shrubs, plants, and forbs that are a mountain meadow is better replaced with a monoculture. Native plants, having survived the rigors of evolution, serve an array of native wildlife. But the stock raisers consider both wild plants and animals worthless, and they replace the vegetation with a tough grass suited for few species but domestic cattle. Public-land stock raisers see their stock and feel their own tradition but not their debt to all Americans. To them the public lands are their ranch, their territory—not a public trust. Many ranchers, after generations of profiting from federal land, are eager today to take it from public ownership.

When public lands were becoming more and more valuable, the "sagebrush rebellion" emerged. It started with people who had long enjoyed dominion over public land-stock raisers and miners—but soon gained the strange bedfellows of free-market economists, political ideologues, and energy corporations.

Early in the Reagan administration, the "sagebrush rebellion's" agenda changed. The objective was clear: the federal lands were to be sold or leased to private interests in a plan called "privatization." The Reagan administration's program to sell vast tracts of "surplus" public lands and energy leases was nothing but a giant transfer of the American public's wealth, power, and freedom to an aristocratic group. The central objective was not just land, but energy resources.

Energy development in the United States followed much the same pattern as timber and other resources. Private stocks of oil and gas were squandered. On public lands conservation was practiced, and the result is that today these lands contain most remaining reserves of oil, gas, oil shale, tar sands, and geothermal resources. Uranium and coal are also there in vast quantities. The greatest economic wealth of the public lands is energy, not the surface rights.

With the remaining energy resources concentrated on them, these lands naturally became the focus of a major energy boom in the early 1980s during the tenure of Secretary of the Interior James G. Watt. The energy corporations embarked on the greatest exploitation program in American history. Watt launched the largest-ever transfer of public resources into private hands—more than $1 trillion's worth. The total impact will not be known for years, but one point is clear: the transfers cheated the public and robbed future generations.

At first glance the "sagebrush rebellion" and the exploitative tactics of the Reagan-Watt administration seem anachronistic after nearly a century of conservation. But a closer look at history reveals that the themes the "sagebrush rebellion" used to plunder public lands are part of a recurring pattern: "worthless" lands become valuable; economic interests create turmoil; and politicians placate special interests. The result has usually been that today's public and future generations lose wealth, power, and freedom.

Four basic themes, which have been with us since the earliest days of the republic, are a constant source of conflict in public-land policy. The first is regionalism. Public lands have pitted one region against another since the Revolutionary War. Small colonies such as Rhode Island and Maryland were afraid of being dominated by large, wealthy colonies such as Virginia and Georgia, which held large western land claims. After the Revolution the practice of opening federally controlled frontier lands to easy settlement worked against the plantation economy of the South. Attempts to industrialize the urban East were blocked when cheap labor migrated to the frontier for an independent life. The political conflict between various regional forces continued until the Civil War, which brought about the Homestead Act. The act shifted control over public-land policy from the South to the frontier and western states, where it has rested ever since.

The regional opposition persisted through the conservation era at the close of the nineteenth century and the beginning of the twentieth century. It was only when eastern-based ideas on conservation were accepted by some western political leaders that large areas were reserved for parks, wildlife refuges, and forests.

Despite the myth, the West has not been a victim of the East; even in conservation and environmental protection the West has controlled the public lands and its own destiny for over a century. Today the theme of regionalism persists as a tension between urban and rural areas. The sparsely populated western outback essentially dictates public-land policy despite urbanization and the political impacts of reapportionment. Urban areas support the operation and management of the public lands through taxes, but the rural regions, led by a minority of ranchers, miners, water developers, and energy companies, dominate the politics and profits. Every year the taxpayers subsidize the stock raisers, miners, loggers, and energy companies operating on the public domain.

The second theme is the historic contrast between aristocratic and democratic uses of land. Originally conflicts over

American land policy arose between the colonists and the English royalty. Soon after the Revolutionary War Thomas Jefferson and Alexander Hamilton emerged as philosophical opponents in debates over federal lands. Hamilton's aristocratic approach favored selling the newly-nationalized land to wealthy speculators and corporations. More democratically, Jefferson and his supporters wanted small land grants with liberal credit for farmers. Even better was the idea of homesteads. The same tensions persisted between the plantation South and the populist West.

Later, when nature's limits were understood and conservation had taken hold in the nineteenth century, public lands essentially became a vast commons. Public land became a territory where all citizens could roam and feel at home on their own estate—their own land. But the economic elitists remained on the public property, and although the lands were purportedly managed for multiple uses, remnants of the old landed aristocracy jealously guarded their traditional profits. The "sagebrush rebels" developed a symbol that was a relic of the western aristocracy steeped in its own mythology of the independent frontier; they captured a macho image reminiscent of the Marlboro Man. They used it to lasso resources for their private profit. The news media, captivated with their own symbols, did not publicize or even understand the opposite side of the conflict—using the land democratically.

A third theme of conflict has been whether to develop the land for economic or social benefits. Economic development has been favored for most of our nation's history. Massive public-land grants were given to a few railroad barons in the nineteenth century. It was not until the 1980 Alaska Lands Act that the amount of land dedicated to national parks and monuments equaled the land given to railroads. More land was given to logging companies than to universities. More land was fraudulently claimed as swamp than was given to all of the war veterans in our history. Despite the "sagebrush rebels'" claims more federal land was granted to states than to homesteaders.

In the 1980s, because a century of conservation has saved resources and rising energy prices have intensified demand for them, we have more public-land wealth at stake than ever before. The primal conflict remains: whether to use land for widespread social purposes or for private economic development.

Finally, the theme of the sharpest conflict is the newest idea, which is a century old: conservation. Early in the history of public lands, little regard was given to conservation. The fall of the buffalo and the thinning and rapid disappearance of clouds of passenger pigeons made the nation apprehensive. Theodore Roosevelt introduced a new public ethic of conservation. He created most of the national forests, established national monuments the size of parks, and enlarged the park system dramatically. Conservation was a major social reform, but like all reforms, it was not completely successful. An archaic group persisted with an old disregard for exhausting natural resources.

The public had become concerned for future resources after seeing the incredible waste and destruction of its lands. But conservation's protection was left incomplete, permitting the public's lands to be plundered anew. Democratic forces retreated, and economic forces became dominant. Conservation for the future public was sacrificed to present private exploitation.

After decades of conservation, public-land management was sharply skewed toward consumptive practices in the early 1980s. It happened with stunning swiftness on an unrivaled scale. Former Secretary of the Interior James Watt renewed the emphasis on consumption. Within months of taking office, he announced he intended to lease virtually all energy resources on the public lands within five years. It was the most massive transfer of public wealth to private hands in history. If the plan were carried out, it would be the final perverse act of an original American sin, the destruction of public land and erosion of the foundation of national strength. The conflict between conservation and development remains bitter.

All Americans share ownership of the immense resources, both physical and spiritual, available from the public's lands. Western public lands represent this nation's best hope to change from the pattern of wasting land, to demonstrate how the human race can use land in harmony with nature. The past and present abuses of these lands must end, but that will happen only when a public trust in federal land is forged into law and seared into a federal land ethic.

Public-land reform is needed because the dream of conserving public resources was never fully built into the land-management mechanisms. Overgrazing exposes soil to wind and erosion. Productive land is lost to desertification. Renewable resources are sacrificed to economic expedience and the search for minerals, oil, and gas.

Reform is needed because of the scandalous transfer of public wealth to private hands. Energy leasing is one massive problem, but every commercial operator and every economic activity on public lands is subsidized by American taxpayers. Timber harvesting reduces wilderness and wildlife habitat while damaging fishing streams and watersheds. Water developers in the West capture public water with federal dams for private use and profit. Mineral development on public lands, controlled by a law written in 1872, remains a blatant subsidy. Reform is needed to end the giveaway of minerals and other resources.

The lands need a manifesto for the future. They should be managed so all citizens can use them democratically as a national heritage and trust. Conserving them for the future, with healthy native vegetation and wildlife, should be the first priority. If their resources are sold, the price must be fair according to the current market to earn the lands' owners a reasonable return. The revenues, particularly from developing nonrenewable resources, should be used to renew the lands and to develop their renewable resources. This program would be part of a national transition to a steady-state economy, which would derive support from the environment without destroying the diversity that stabilizes life and assures a productive living system for all generations. This is not the direction of current management programs.

In the 1980s the public lands as people have known them during the twentieth century are facing the largest looting in American history. The democratic purposes for which the lands were reserved are endangered. The lands' wealth—and therefore power—is being transferred to a few people and corporations with political clout. The essential American freedom of open land is being diminished. The liberty that comes from public land is fading like a winter sunset.

Land reform is usually the product of epic historic forces and revolutions in the land's use. It is ironic that reforming land management is crucial, because managing public land for the people's benefit is a constant theme of democracy, and abusing the public-land trust is a product of dictatorial instincts. Land reform is generally associated with banana republics, not the United States; yet federal lands here have been seized and looted by powerful economic and political forces, and the public trust is being lost. Nothing less than national reform can restore the values and the resources of federal lands to their rightful owners, the American people.

Writing a manifesto for the public lands will require a perspective that protects the interests of the entire nation over many generations. Public land must be shared with our future citizens; protecting and enhancing it are gifts from this generation to the next. The reform should also end economic subsidies and control by special-interest groups. Non-economic uses of public lands must take precedence over economic activities. Developing renewable resources must be preferred to developing nonrenewable resources. Public values on public land should have priority over private development.

Federal lands are a treasure, not just an amenity or a capital resource. All people of this nation have a basic inalienable right to use and enjoy them. Public lands are a freedom. They are essential to a democratic nation and the spiritual strength of its people.

The beauty of the public's lands and the drama of their history conjure visions of space and openness. The lands draw the eye to the horizon. The sky is clearer there and the horizon wider. Most public lands are in the West, where thin, dry, unpolluted air lets the sun shine brighter and the sky look bluer than anywhere else in the country. Public lands define the region more than literature, art, accent, or cowboy boots. The West of history, movies, myths, and dreams cannot be found in Denver or Los Angeles, but only on the lands the people own. Open land and western space are gifts of the vision and dreams that helped create the nation. Every person, every generation needs to believe in something tangible that is anchored to the past and will extend into the future. Protecting and perpetuating the lands that embody this vision is a trust that was given to this generation; it is a sacred trust in the lands we all own, and we must pass it on to our children.

What Threatens Our National Wildlife Refuge System?

The policy of setting aside land for the specific purpose of protecting wildlife was first put into action by President Theodore Roosevelt. In 1903, he established the first National Wildlife Refuge (NWR) on Pelican Island in Florida. Pelican Island became a refuge for thousands of birds being threatened by hunters who wanted to sell their showy feathers. Today, the National Wildlife Refuge system includes 92 million acres across 50 states and several overseas territories. It protects thousands of species of animals. Of these, 282 species are either threatened or endangered.[1]

Refuges include a great variety of habitats. Examples include the cypress swamps of the Okefenokee NWR in Florida, prairie potholes (known as the "duck factories" of North America) of the Arrowwood NWR in North Dakota, and the Arctic NWR in Alaska.

In addition to the primary purpose of protecting lands, water, and wildlife, refuges have been shown to provide another benefit. According to an October 2003 press release by the U.S. Fish and Wildlife Service, more than 35 million people who visited refuges in 2002 contributed over $809 million to local economies through sales of recreation, equipment, food, lodging, transportation, and related expenses. That figure reflects over twice as much as was generated in 1995, the date of the previous study. The total money generated from sales and tourism related to the refuges, not including Alaska and Hawaii, totaled $1.12 billion.[2]

However, as the following article demonstrates, U.S. national wildlife refuges are still under threat. Sometimes the dangers come from resource extraction. Threats also come from outside the refuges. People divert refuge water for use in cities and for irrigation. Pollution from urban growth makes its way into the refuges' land, water, and air. Funding to manage the refuge system is often not enough to meet the management needs.

Having just celebrated its 100th birthday, the National Wildlife Refuge system has received a lot of attention. As

U.S. environmental policies continue to evolve, it remains to be seen whether they will adequately protect the huge financial and biological resources that reside in the 540 National Wildlife Refuges.

—The Editor

1. Graham, Frank, Jr. "Where Wildlife Rules." *Audubon*. June 2003.

2. U.S. Fish and Wildlife Service Press Release. October 9, 2003. Available online at *http://mountain-prairie.fws.gov/pressrel/03-79.htm*.

The Greatest Show on Earth
by Jessica Snyder Sachs

The numbers are extraordinary by any measure: more than 700 species of birds, 220 mammals, 250 reptiles and amphibians, at least 200 fish and countless varieties of insects and plants. America's National Wildlife Refuge System provides sanctuaries for most of the native species that fly, run, walk, slither, swim and take root in this country. It is the world's largest network of public lands and waters set aside specifically for the protection of wildlife. And on the eve of its 100th anniversary on March 14, refuge managers have much to celebrate. But as this issue's articles explain, they also face some serious challenges in the years ahead.

THE EARLY MORNING SUN glints off the amber, "swamp tea" waters of Okefenokee National Wildlife Refuge, as an eager group of Sunday birders clamber up its wetland observation tower. For the last half mile of boardwalk, they've heard the croak of sandhill cranes above the rustling sound of the sawgrass blocking their view. "They'll be lifting off any day now," says refuge ranger Maggie O'Connell of the swamp's winter population of several thousand greater sandhill cranes. Though only mid-February, winter is already loosening its halfhearted grip on southern Georgia's Great Okefenokee, one of the largest intact freshwater ecosystems in the world.

Atop the 50-foot tower, O'Connell surveys her domain. "Seventeen miles to the horizon without a stitch of solid ground," she marvels. Indeed, the dense vegetation of this landscape grows atop floating peat-bog islands, the largest crowned by bald cypress draped in ghostly green Spanish moss. For good reason, the Creek Indians dubbed this Oguafenogua, the "land of the trembling earth." Stomp hard enough and even the trees shake.

Like the majority of the 539 units in America's National Wildlife Refuge System, the Okefenokee was protected to serve as sanctuary for migratory waterfowl such as the cranes, teals, mergansers, herons and egrets seen feeding across its open, wet "prairie." But the Georgia reserve has evolved far beyond its "duck factory" genesis.

This refuge's expanded purpose becomes clear as the sun rises high enough to banish the morning chill, and boaters begin paddling and motoring up the swamp's 120 miles of canals and slow-moving streams. Blinking back at them from the shore or half-submerged in the shimmering blackwater are the sleek American alligators that are among the Okefenokee's star attractions. Many of the visitors will linger after returning to dock—lunching on the refuge's grassy picnic grounds, touring its new million-dollar environmental education exhibit, and shopping for souvenirs in the gift shop. Some will spend the night, either in the state park easement on the refuge's west side or deep in the swamp, on one of seven overnight canoeing platforms.

In addition to playing host to more than 400,000 visitors a year, the staff of this national wildlife refuge have launched an ambitious long-term project to restore and expand the area's upland stands of rare longleaf pine and wiregrass habitat—home to endangered red-cockaded woodpeckers and threatened gopher tortoises, indigo snakes and Florida black bears. To this end, nearly half the refuge staff work on the fire crews that conduct prescribed burns to beat back the saw palmetto and slash pine that once were kept in check by seasonal wildfires. "We figure it'll take about 300 years of active management to restore the area," says O'Connell.

Now, as it prepares to celebrate its centennial year beginning in March [2003], the National Wildlife Refuge System as a whole is experiencing an equally radical deepening and expansion of its purpose. Administered by the U.S. Fish and Wildlife Service, it is the world's only national network of public lands set aside specifically for wildlife. And for years, it struggled without any sense of unifying mission. Beginning with President Theodore Roosevelt's founding of the first refuge—Florida's Pelican Island in 1903—one unit after another has flickered into being with its own narrowly defined mission. Before Roosevelt left office in 1909, these included 56 big game preserves and bird reservations such as Idaho's Mindoka refuge for ducks and geese, Oklahoma's Wichita Mountains for bison and elk, and Alaska's Fire Island for moose.

Since 1934, the Migratory Bird Hunting and Conservation Stamp Act has funded the acquisition of millions of acres of additional waterfowl habitat, concentrated up and down North America's four major migratory flyways. Among the first, Montana's Red Rock Lakes refuge became the last-chance sanctuary for the highly endangered trumpeter swan in 1935.

In 1966, Congress passed the National Wildlife Refuge Administration Act, enlarging the refuge system further with several thousand small prairie pothole wetlands designated as "Waterfowl Production Areas." And in 1980, the Alaska National Interest Lands Conservation Act nearly tripled the refuge system's holdings with some 54 million acres of pristine arctic and subarctic habitat.

By the time the 500th refuge—West Virginia's Canaan Valley—was established in 1994, the system encompassed more units than the National Forest Service and more land (90 million acres) than the National Park Service's holdings. Yet much of the refuge system continued to be managed under a mishmash of policies and regulations that left its lands vulnerable to such strangely incompatible uses as jet skiing, dune-buggy racing, livestock grazing, oil drilling, even military war games and bombing runs. Refuge managers opposing such uses stood on shaky legal ground unless they could show that the activities directly threatened the specific purpose for which their refuges had been established.

A case in point: In 1990, the manager of Aransas National Wildlife Refuge on the Texas Gulf Coast tried to remove privately owned cattle from the preserve's wildlife-rich Matagorda Island. Biologists had determined that overgrazing had already degraded the island's otherwise pristine habitat, including nesting sites for endangered sea turtles and underbrush vital to wintering songbirds. The problem was that Congress had established the refuge in 1937 specifically as a sanctuary for the world's last wild population of whooping cranes.

"We could show that the cattle were definitely degrading the overall ecosystem of Matagorda Island," explains National Wildlife Refuge System Director Dan Ashe. "But technically, in order to deny the grazing permit, we had to show that it was incompatible with the refuge's original purpose." In the end, federal administrators stood behind the refuge manager's claim that cattle grazing constituted an incompatible use. "But a lot of people, including our own attorneys, thought we were stretching things," admits Ashe.

Such legalistic hand-tying came to an end in 1996, with an executive order by President [Bill] Clinton, followed the next year by the bipartisan passage of the National Wildlife Refuge System Improvement Act. These two legal directives set forth "conservation" as the refuge system's singular and all-encompassing purpose—a purpose against which any proposed use had to be judged.

The groundbreaking Improvement Act also required the staff at every refuge to create a 15-year comprehensive conservation plan—guided, in large part, by public input. Indeed, by placing an emphasis on "wildlife-compatible" uses such as observation, photography and limited hunting, the law acknowledged that refuges are for people too.

Specifically, some 2 million hunters and 6 million anglers visit the refuge system each year. Twice that number—some 16 million visitors—come solely to watch wildlife or soak in the beauty and serenity of the nation's wildest places. Add busloads of students and tour groups taking advantage of environmental education programs and the tally swells to at least 35 million visitors a year. The importance of their input in setting the system's agenda for its second century can hardly be underestimated, says Jamie Rappaport Clark, former director of the U.S. Fish and Wildlife Service during the Clinton administration and now NWF senior vice president for conservation programs.

"The pressures on the refuge system have grown tremendously in recent years," she explains. "We have more threatened and endangered species, more demands for human activity on the landscape, and more development and encroachment from the outside. As a result, the job of safeguarding these wild places and passing them on to new generations demands a high level of public engagement."

In fact, the most serious threats to refuge wildlife and habitat—urban sprawl, water depletion, pollution and invasive species—originate outside refuge borders and, therefore beyond the system's authority. Consequently, progress depends on activism on the part of local citizens and allied conservation organizations.

In recent years, for example, the Okefenokee National Wildlife Refuge has depended on a large coalition of conservation groups, including NWF and its affiliate, the Georgia Wildlife Federation, to stave off plans by the chemical giant DuPont to excavate a 30-mile-long, 50-foot-deep titanium strip mine a few feet from the refuge's eastern border. The proposed mining operations would generate a 24-hour-a-day onslaught of dust, smoke, exhaust, noise and light directly alongside the refuge's main wildlife observation drive. Worse, scientific studies indicate the mine could irrevocably alter the Okefenokee's delicate hydrology and ecology. With no authority to stop operations off refuge grounds, refuge managers continue to rely on sustained and vocal public opposition to keep DuPont's plans at bay.

Public opposition has, at least for the time being, helped play an even larger role in confronting what many people view as the greatest single threat to the refuge system in its 100-year history: the proposed opening of the coastal plain section of Alaska's 19.6 million-acre Arctic National Wildlife Refuge to oil drilling—a plan that the U.S. Senate voted down last year [2002]. Scientific studies by government wildlife biologists had confirmed that petroleum operations on the Arctic refuge would disrupt its vast caribou calving grounds and irreparably harm the region's delicate tundra ecosystem. More importantly, says Clark, "opening Arctic to drilling would totally blow apart the purpose of the entire refuge system. For if there's the will to violate a refuge as spectacular and ecologically unique as Arctic, what would stop the same from happening at the system's 75 million other acres?"

At the least, adds Clark, the 1997 Refuge Improvement Act makes doing so extremely difficult. "As there's no possible way to open up the heart of this refuge to drilling and call it 'compatible' with conservation," she says, "it would require Congressional legislation to literally set the Refuge Improvement Act aside."

More insidious threats to the system include a widening budget shortfall for staffing and maintenance, says Evan Hirsche, president of the National Wildlife Refuge Association, the umbrella organization for more than 200 local refuge volunteer "friends" groups. "Wildlife refuges have long been the black sheep of federal land holdings in terms of monetary support," he says. Specifically, the system must manage more than 94 million acres—and the welfare of more than 200 threatened or endangered species—with an annual budget of $370 million, or less than $4 an acre.

"As a result," says Hirsche, "a great deal of conservation objectives are not being met." Primary among these has been the refuge system's losing battle with invasive species such as the Australian pine and Brazilian pepper trees supplanting native habitat at Florida's Pelican Island National Wildlife Refuge; the zebra mussels and purple loosestrife crowding out native mollusks and wetland plant species in the Upper Mississippi National Fish and Wildlife Refuge; and nutria, a beaver-like Central American rodent, tearing up tidal marshes in Maryland's Blackwater National Wildlife Refuge. Also showing the strain of underfunding is the refuge system's aging infrastructure of access roads, buildings, water-management facilities and other assets.

The severe underfunding for maintenance and staff has also slowed the system's opening of new refuges, despite the annual influx of "Duck Stamp" money for land acquisition. "Before we acquire new areas, we have to ask ourselves whether we'll have the funds to manage them," explains Ashe. "Too often, I hear the argument, 'You don't have to do anything, just buy the land and protect it.' But 'protect' is an active verb."

Indeed, though much of the refuge system consists of wilderness where humans seldom tread, at a minimum, these places must be posted and patrolled. "In this day and age, even our most remote areas are no longer insulated from such illegal activities as drug trafficking, poaching and garbage dumping," says Ashe. "If we just left these places alone, I don't think anyone would be happy with what we'd find when we came back five years later."

Moreover, a large percentage of the refuge system requires intensive management such as controlled burning to maintain ecosystem balance and active farming to provide grain for migratory waterfowl. "We need more maintenance workers, more equipment operators, more law-enforcement officers," says Ashe.

In particular, Ashe and conservation activists agree, the system needs more wildlife biologists. "The lack of biological expertise undermines any effort at strategic planning and wise management," says Clark. "Many of our refuges need extensive habitat restoration that can't be carried out because of this lack of biological expertise." At the very least, she explains, the system needs enough biologists to conduct wildlife surveys, monitor wildlife threats and prioritize spending at individual refuges.

For all these reasons, a coalition of 20 conservation groups, including the National Wildlife Federation, recently called on President [George W.] Bush and Congress to nearly double the refuge system's budget. "Because of their strategic locations and acreage, our refuges provide safe havens for hundreds of threatened and endangered species, provide migratory stopover for millions of birds, while at the same time provide terrific areas for solace and enjoyment for people who want to experience nature," argues Clark. "But it's a system that desperately requires increased funding if it's going to address the needs of both wildlife and people."

The good news is that authorities in Washington, D.C., are finally getting the message. "We've seen sustained budget increases over recent years, including Secretary of the Interior Gale Norton's endorsement of a nearly $57 million increase for maintenance and operations in 2003," says Ashe, who credits conservation groups for their persistent lobbying on behalf of the refuge system. "Constituent organizations like the National Wildlife Federation have in the past five to six years rallied to our defense. It's in large part thanks to them that government leaders have been able to set aside political differences and support us."

Admittedly, recent federal funding increases fall far short of the refuge system's staggering maintenance backlog—currently estimated at more than $526 million, with another $700 million needed for high-priority projects such as restoring degraded habitats and promoting the recovery of endangered species.

Increasingly, refuges have come to rely on volunteers to pick up the slack. Every year some 30,000 volunteers donate more than a million hours of their time to driving heavy equipment, conducting habitat surveys, building boardwalks, running bookstores and nature programs, and lobbying for increased local, state and federal support. "That translates to about $13 million worth of services a year," notes Hirsche.

The need for volunteer support will only increase in the refuge system's second century. "These precious places are mere islands in the landscape, and we can't hope to ever acquire all the land we need," he explains. "As a result, the success of the system's conservation mission will depend on local volunteers becoming envoys to neighboring landowners and local governments, and in this way extending each refuge's wildlife objectives beyond its borders."

In the future that Hirsche envisions, "refuges will become shining examples for private landowners, state land managers and other federal land agencies of how they can all develop management policies consistent with species conservation."

How Do Marine Reserves Protect Ocean Resources?

The United States became the first country to establish a policy of protecting special lands by creating Yellowstone National Park in 1872. It took 100 years for the protection policy to make its way to coastal waters, but in 1972, Congress established the National Marine Sanctuary program. Thirteen marine sanctuaries have been created since then, protecting an area of nearly 18,000 square miles of ocean waters. This represents an area about the size of the states of New Hampshire and Vermont combined.[1] Marine sanctuaries include breeding and feeding grounds of whales, sea lions, and sea turtles; coral reefs and kelp forests; and the underwater remains of the U.S.S. *Monitor*, a Civil War ship.

Marine Sanctuaries are managed to protect ecological and historical resources. Many activities, such as sport and commercial fishing, are allowed. A higher level of protection is given to much smaller areas designated as marine reserves, established within the sanctuaries, as "no-take" areas. Regulations prohibit the taking of all marine life, do not allow the discharge of cooling water or engine exhaust, and ban the anchoring of boats. People may snorkel and dive if they obtain a free permit first. The purpose is to protect these highly sensitive and valuable ocean resources.

The following article examines the increasing interest in expanding the marine reserve program. A 151-square-mile reserve, the Tortugas Ecological Reserve in the Florida Keys National Marine Sanctuary, was created in 2001. The program is the result of many different interest groups working together. The site was added to the network of 23 no-take zones in the sanctuary.[2] Though people may be skeptical at first of protecting marine areas, many note the economic benefits as they see the fish populations and habitats rebound.[3] In fact, polls conducted among residents showed that 78% supported no-take zones in the Florida Keys.[4] Healthy reefs provide billions of dollars in reef-related activities in several Florida counties alone.[5]

Other marine areas are being considered for additional protection. The Channel Islands National Marine Sanctuary Advisory

Council is considering setting up marine reserves in California. As the fishermen in New England have learned from a failing fishing industry, the ocean is not a resource without limits. Just as we protect species and habitats in our national parks, the time to protect the lands that lie beneath the oceans has arrived.

—The Editor

1. National Oceanic and Atmospheric Administration (NOAA). *Florida Keys National Marine Sanctuary*. 2003. Available online at *http://www.fknms.nos .noaa.gov/tortugas/*.

2. National Oceanic and Atmospheric Administration (NOAA). *Welcome to Marine Sanctuaries*. 2004. Available online at *http://www.sanctuaries.nos.noaa.gov/*.

3. Klingener, Nancy. "Providing Sanctuary." *Blue Planet*. Fall 2002.

4. "Socioeconomic Study of Reefs in Southeast Florida." 2001. Available online at *http://marineeconomics.noaa.gov/Reefs/02-01.pdf*.

5. Ibid.

Undiscovered Country
by David Helvarg

In the future, America's national parks won't just be on land; they'll also be under the waves. California is leading the way.

I was snorkeling the warm, clear waters of the Dry Tortugas off Florida last summer, just as a hard-won deal to turn it into the largest fully protected area of underwater America was being clinched. Shimmering shoals of baitfish, schools of blue-and-yellow striped grunts, and haughty-looking queen angelfish the size of saucepans swam past me. There were brain and rock corals, branching staghorn, and lacy sea fans. I spotted a five-foot nurse shark, and held my breath to hear the big aqua-green, red, and purple parrot fish grazing contentedly on the coral. Above the surface, squadrons of chevron-tailed frigate birds patrolled, searching for flying fish and other easy pickings.

Dry Tortugas is 151 square nautical miles (soon to be 197) in which fishing, drilling, dumping, treasure hunting, and anchor dragging are no longer allowed. Nor is any other activity that threatens the natural wonder of the place, which offers its visitors the genuine National Geo[graphic] experience. You can come to snorkel, sail, or dive. But take only pictures and leave only bubbles.

If all goes well, Dry Tortugas may be only the first of a string of new underwater wilderness parks. There are projects now afoot to establish fully protected ocean areas in the Gulf of Maine, off Washington State, and elsewhere. But the most promising effort—and the most contentious battle—is taking shape in California. The state already has a few small marine reserves, just two-tenths of 1 percent of its coastal waters. Now, a pro-conservation coalition is trying to win enough popular support to create what could one day be the nation's most complete network of underwater wilderness.

Yes, wilderness. "I am glad I shall never be young without wild country to be young in," Aldo Leopold once wrote. "Of what avail are forty freedoms without a blank spot on the map?"

As terrestrial beings, we tend to forget that most of our planet's surface remains a blank spot. We've mapped less than 5 percent of our oceans with the accuracy we've achieved in mapping 100 percent of the moon. We're only now discovering and exploring previously unknown ecosystems, such as deep-ocean coral forests, hydrothermal vent communities, and the craggy slopes of submarine mountains. Yet the oceans contain more than 80 percent of all species and 95 percent of all livable habitat. They represent a second chance to do right by the wilderness that gave birth to us all.

In 1890 the U.S. Census Bureau declared the American frontier closed. But in 1983 Ronald Reagan, in one of his most significant and least noted acts, created a new frontier. Following international precedent, he established a 200-mile-wide Exclusive Economic Zone stretching out from America's shores, a wild new territory six times the size of the Louisiana Purchase.

For the most part, we've continued to treat this blue frontier much as we treated our original frontier—as a place to drill for oil, dump our wastes, and slaughter wildlife. In 2000, however, a National Academy of Sciences report called for wilderness protection for a fifth of America's coastal waters, in order to sustain dwindling fisheries and wildlife populations. Bill Clinton then issued an executive order establishing the framework for a national system of protected marine areas. He also created the Northwestern Hawaiian Islands Ecosystem Reserve, a vast oceanic extension of the island chain.

But in the mangrove tangle of overlapping jurisdictions and special interests that governs offshore management, protecting ocean wilderness may prove even more challenging than protecting terrestrial wilderness.

"You have to balance the interests of the environmentalists with our right to make a living," says Bob Fletcher, the tall, trim, gray-eyed president of the Sportfishing Association of California. We're at a sport fishing landing on San Diego Bay, and the docks behind Fletcher are lined with dozens of big party boats emblazoned with names like *Top Gun*, *Prowler*, and *Conquest*.

Recreational ocean fishing is big business in California. In the aggregate, Fletcher and his colleagues make $2.5 billion a year taking their clients out to hunt fish with sonar. The industry has responded to steep declines in California fisheries by redefining trophy fish. In the 1960s, for instance, mackerel was used as bait. Now that many of the big fish are gone, mackerel is on the industry's list of daily catches. The recreational fishing industry doesn't sell fish, however. It sells the "experience" of fishing. And many of its clients lack the long-term perspective to notice the changes.

"I think reserves will decrease rather than increase yields," Fletcher tells me. He argues that closing an area of the ocean to fishing means closing off its contribution to the catch, and he claims that traditional management can restore fisheries. "If we get reserves at the levels environmentalists want," he warns, "you'll devastate opportunities for recreational fisheries and anglers."

What has Fletcher so concerned is the state's Marine Life Protection Act. Originally supported by NRDC [Natural Resources Defense Council], the Orange County Marine

Institute, and other conservation and marine education groups, it was celebrated as a major environmental victory when it became law in 1999. The act called for the creation of a large network of fully protected areas along the state's 1,100-mile coastline by June 2002.

That's not going to happen. In July 2001 the Department of Fish and Game released initial maps of the planned reserves. But the maps had been put together with little input from the fishing sector or other stakeholders among the general public—an act of political bumbling that set off a series of angry public hearings. The deadline was rolled back to December 2003.

Today, California is in the midst of a public comment period in which the state must gather input from stakeholders and use it to redraw the maps. The sport fishing industry is the leading force pushing for minimal reserves. "Let's not alienate everyone," Fletcher says. "Let's start small, move [the reserves] away from the coast, and document them over five to ten years."

It occurs to me that if either side isn't satisfied with the state's final recommendations, they might sue. Wouldn't the result be years of additional delay, I ask Fletcher, with the reserves tied up in court indefinitely?

"I don't see that as such a bad thing," he says, grinning. "I'm not against inaction."

"There's always been this 'out-of-sight, out-of-mind' thinking about the sea," says Gary Davis, senior scientist at the Channel Islands National Park. "Now we're beginning to understand how people can have devastating effects on marine productivity. We're fragmenting marine habitats to where they're not viable."

I'm meeting with the big, sun-burnished scientist at the park headquarters by the Ventura harbor. Davis is stout, casual, and authoritative, and watching him, I can't help thinking of the skipper on "Gilligan's Island."

The Channel Islands Park, off southern California, is half on land—five windy, rugged islands—and half underwater. The most famous of its marine ecosystems are forests of giant kelp, often called underwater rainforests because they shelter so many species. But even though this is a national park, fishing is permitted in most of it. Since 1999 there have been proposals to greatly expand the park's few no-take reserves. While the political process creeps on, however, the fishing continues.

"We're losing species like abalone and rockfish," Davis laments. "The predators and large grazers are being fished out. Then, when you have storms taking out the kelp, you discover it's only in the reserves that the kelp forests consistently recover. Because the red urchins and lobsters, and big sheephead and abalones, are still there, keeping the system in balance."

I'm distracted by the view out his office window. Across the wind-whipped Santa Barbara Channel are the Channel Islands—where six-foot waves mean there's no way I can scuba-dive Anacapa Island's famous 37-acre reserve today.

I know what I'm missing. I've dived in a few of California's other small cold-water reserves, including Point Lobos, south of Monterey, where I've seen cathedral shafts of sunlight playing through the giant kelp forests. Kelp gardens have an otherworldly, hidden-forest feel. There are translucent stalks and leaves rising above seafloors littered with strawberry anemones, starfish, urchins, and abalones. There are big, spiny, bug-eyed rockfish, so ugly they're attractive. There are sea otters, seals, and sea lions, sometimes checking you out as if they were acrobatic jocks. On rare occasions, there is a great white shark—the definitive sign of a productive ecosystem. As naturalist Ed Abbey said: "If there's not something bigger and meaner than you are out there, it's not really a wilderness."

Gary Davis thinks most fishermen and fisherwomen will become converts to reserves once they see the "spillover" effect in action. As large fish and other creatures start to thrive in the protected areas, he explains, they migrate out—often right to the traps, nets, and hooks of the fishing boats.

A few days later, at the La Jolla Cove reserve some 200 miles to the south, I see what he means. Just past the yellow buoys at the edge of the reserve, the sea is thick with marker floats for lobster traps. Clearly, lobster fishers have noticed that the fishing is good right by the protected zone.

There's plenty of evidence to back them up. The first large-scale study of marine ecological reserves, released at the 2001 annual meeting of the American Association for the Advancement of Science, found higher densities of fish, larger animals, and greater biodiversity in no-take zones. In Florida, world-record catches of three species of sport fish occurred more frequently near Cape Canaveral (off-limits since 1962 for national security reasons) than in all the rest of the state combined. At Georges Bank, a New England fishing ground closed in 1994 due to catastrophic overfishing, the scallop population has grown fourteen-fold, and haddock, yellowtail flounder, and other species have rebounded.

Interestingly, California's commercial fishing industry hasn't been as vocal in opposing reserves as the state's recreational fishing industry. One reason may be that commercial fishermen and fisherwomen are effectively the top predators in the marine ecosystem. When the prey disappear, they feel it. "We're killing them with our electronics [fish-finding sonar]," one disgruntled fisherman in Bodega Bay tells me. "The fishing grounds are like freeways now, and we're just wiping them out."

"Some of our members say, 'Don't agree to anything,'" says Zeke Grader, president of the Pacific Coast Federation of Fishermen's Associations, a commercial fishing group. "But I tell them that if we do right by the resource, we do right by our industry. If you get fishermen involved, they'll be the ones promoting new reserves and feeling the scientists and others are working for them."

California environmentalists are cautiously optimistic about the fate of the Marine Life Protection Act. NRDC's Karen Garrison has seen even the loudest public meetings "get constructive" when fishermen and fisherwomen, conservationists, and scientists come together in smaller groups to discuss specifics. What's more, other constituencies are becoming more involved.

On a cool December evening, I attend a meeting of San Diego's Council of Divers. Some three dozen burly recreational divers, men and women in denim, wool, and fleece, have gathered to hear a talk on marine reserves by Scripps Institution of Oceanography scientist Paul Dayton. When Dayton shows a slide of a juvenile abalone hiding under a red urchin, the crowd "Awwws" its appreciation. Only divers could find a baby abalone cute, I think.

Dayton calls the kelp forests of today "ghost forests," because so many of their inhabitants are missing—giant black sea bass, big lobsters, moray eels, billfish. He has slides from a few decades ago showing lobsters the size of bulldogs and black sea bass larger than the men who caught them.

"I just don't see why there is such opposition to these reserves," Dayton tells the divers. "In Western Australia, [lobster] fishermen are demanding larger reserves because they're making so much money off the spillover."

One diver wonders whether he will ever be able to collect abs [abalones] in his lifetime. Another speaks of growing up near beaches that were covered with shells when she was a child—but are no longer.

After Dayton's presentation, the president of the council (the only diver wearing a sports jacket) stands up. He asks the group's members to voice their opinions to California's Fish and Game Commission. Tell other members to get involved, he says.

These are only three dozen people, but they represent some 1,500 local divers. In turn, San Diego's divers are just a sliver of the far larger, disparate group of ocean enthusiasts I've encountered who support reserves, from Paul Dayton to week-end swimmers. They are becoming a true grassroots political force in the state—and across the country. I like to call them the Seaweed Rebellion: scientists, surfers, coastal residents, fishermen and fisherwomen, divers, businesspeople, environmentalists, and others, committing to do the right thing for the living seas they love.

The oceans, after all, have given life to our planet. They are the drivers of climate and weather. They give us almost three-fourths of the oxygen we need. Our bodies, like the planet, are

71 percent water; our blood is exactly as salty as the sea. Going to the beach is our number-one outdoor recreational activity.

Giving back a little in the form of marine wilderness would seem the least we could do. Henry David Thoreau wrote, "Heaven is under our feet as well as over our heads. . . . We need the tonic of wilderness." I'd just amend that to say: Heaven is also under our flippers.

What Are Some Public Land Issues?

It is a question as old as the United States itself: Who should be allowed to use federal lands? Are there some federal lands that should be protected from development? Should oil companies and timber companies be permitted to extract profits from the land, leaving behind potential environmental problems? Who should decide? As the country continues to require more coal, gas, oil, and timber to fuel the activities of everyday life, these questions become more and more important.

Some people believe that mining laws developed over 100 years ago no longer address the environmental concerns we have today. After observing the environmental problems caused by oil and timber companies, some people no longer want them to extract resources from environmentally sensitive federal lands. Other people, however, argue that the country needs the gas, oil, and timber, and that federal lands should be used to meet these public needs.

The following article captures the federal land use issues in the discussion of a current battle over land use rights in Montana. An area known as the Rocky Mountain Front is home to the "last intact viable assemblage of large carnivores in the Lower 48 [states] as well as viable populations of 10 native big game animals." The executive director of the Montana Petroleum Association tried to assure people that, "We aren't going to screw up the land." But some residents look at other sites with oil and mining wastes and too many roads cutting across the habitats needed by large mammals like elk, deer, big horn sheep, and bear, and doubt that drilling, roads, and pipelines will have as little impact as the oil company claims.

It is a story being played out as well on other federal lands on which the U.S. Forest Service sells oil and mining leases. Some government administrations, like those of Ronald Reagan and George W. Bush, pursue policies of opening up federal lands to drilling and timber. Sometimes public outcry, however, stops the leasing process. For example, recent public protest against the idea of drilling in the Arctic National Wildlife Refuge caused the House of Representatives and Senate to defeat the proposal. Still, the debate is far from over.

—The Editor

Frontal Assault
by Joel Connelly

Grizzlies and other wildlife may well bear the brunt of plans to tap into the resources of the untamed Rocky Mountain Front.

Of the wild North America traveled by Meriwether Lewis and William Clark two centuries ago, one place remains that they would still recognize: the Rocky Mountain Front.

When he first spied the Rockies, Lewis wrote of his "joy" and "secret pleasure," but shuddered in anticipation of the "sufferings and hardships" his party would encounter there. Today, the Front remains wild, ruggedly beautiful country, rising abruptly from the Montana plains—a mountain rampart of sharp, barren peaks that stretches from the Canadian border 100 miles south to Helena. Heading west from Great Falls, a visitor can step back in time to an American West not yet drilled, clear-cut or subdivided. But all that will pass away if plans for oil and gas drilling on public lands throughout the Front get under way.

The Front ranks in the top 1 percent of U.S. wildlife habitat, according to Mike Aderhold, a regional supervisor for Montana's Department of Fish, Wildlife and Parks. It holds the last intact viable assemblage of large carnivores in the Lower 48 [states] as well as viable populations of 10 native big game animals. Seven of Montana's 14 threatened and endangered species inhabit the Front, along with 21 species of breeding raptors, tens of thousands of migrating snow geese and a third of the plants known in Montana, including 18 sensitive plant species.

"It is an area truly unique for the diversity of its wildlife," says Nathan Birkeland of the Montana Wildlife Federation, an

NWF [National Wildlife Federation] affiliate that serves as an umbrella group for 25 hunting, fishing and outdoor clubs in the Big Sky State. "It is home to 290 species, the country's second-largest elk herd and its biggest population of bighorn sheep. Nowhere else does the grizzly bear roam on the plains. All of these species are able to stay where they have been for millennia. In the mountains you have wilderness. At the edge of the plains you have large ranches and not a lot of subdivision."

The Front's 3,000 elk share the region with at least as many deer, and the area is one of the last places below Canada where bighorn graze on the plains. More than 100 grizzly bears and 300 to 400 black bears roam the Front. Virtually exterminated in the region early in the last century, wolves have recolonized the Front, coming south from Canada without human intervention. The mountain lion population is thriving there, as are wolverines and Canada lynx.

But for many of these animals, parts of the Rocky Mountain Front soon may cease to provide a pristine home. The Bush administration is concocting plans to remodel the Front, putting oil and gas wells on thousands of acres of Bureau of Land Management (BLM) and U.S. Forest Service lands—in most cases, sensitive slopes and benches where mountains give way to plains. And the administration wants quick action: It has directed federal managers to remove regulatory obstacles to oil and gas development along the Front, speeding up the authorization of wells. Managers have been told that any delays in drilling will have to be justified specifically. Concern for wildlife and its habitat is no longer a priority.

During the 2000 campaign, vice-presidential candidate Dick Cheney liked to lecture reporters on new techniques for recovering natural gas. He boasted of the "tiny footprint" being left on the land by new wells in his native Wyoming. Lately, reassuring words like his have come from BLM director Kathleen Clark: "Our overall objective is to ensure the timely development of these critical energy resources in an environmentally sound manner." Gail Abercrombie, executive director of the Montana Petroleum Association, has made a similar pitch, recently telling *The Washington Post*, "We aren't going to screw up the land. The grizzly bears and elk will be there with natural gas production. It is not one or the other. We will have both."

Conservative, largely Republican rural residents along the Front aren't buying the administration line. They have seen how pipelines and roads and seismic lines have made southwest Alberta "look like a fishnet," according to Barrie Gilbert, wildlife biologist and senior scientist at Utah State University. Gilbert has studied gas drilling and its consequences extensively. "Roads go out to all the well sites," says Gilbert. "Power is needed, and the lines often don't follow the road path. You need pumps, collectors. If a well is successful, a pipeline is needed to take gas from the site. It will connect to another pipeline. All these lines of access are vulnerable to off-road vehicles, which in turn means poaching."

Quantifying is difficult, but Brian Horejsi of Western Wildlife Environmental Consulting in Calgary, who has written extensively about impacts on wildlife, estimates that each new well requires at least a mile or two of new road. Shell Oil once promised that only a single pipeline would cross a ranch adjoining the company's plant in Pincher Creek, near Canada's Waterton Lakes National Park. "You now see 10 separate pipelines on the property," Horejsi says.

The plant—set amidst lands still largely rural and publicly owned—has caused chills among Montanans fearful that similar industrialization is headed their way. It sends toxic pollutants into the atmosphere, has a high volume of truck traffic and a sizeable workforce. "The place is totally a mess, totally out of hand," says Roy Jacobs, a taxidermist in Choteau.

R. L. "Stoney" Burk, a lawyer who has practiced for 21 years in Choteau, is a decorated former fighter pilot, avid hunter and core conservative in his suspicion of government power. The fight over the Front has, in Burk's words, turned him into "a very angry ex-Republican." Not only does Burk look north to the roads and pipelines coming out of Alberta canyons, but he also gazes over the Rockies to the mining wastes and Superfund cleanup sites in western Montana. Industrial development has left a terrible legacy across the state, from contaminated soils over a 5-square-mile site in Butte (and lead dust in local attics) to contaminated groundwater in Anaconda. Asbestos contamination continues to claim the lives of workers and family members at the shut-down W. R. Grace vermiculite mine in Libby.

"Time after time, in today's world, the mining companies have stepped on our faces and left us with multimillion-dollar cleanups," Burk says. "They've done it to Montana again and again. I fear the same with gas development. If they hit [gas], they walk away with millions of dollars. What do we get? Scars on the land, and a very short-term economic benefit. We get potential toxification of our water supplies. We get roads built, which opens the potential for poaching. The reason you have all these animals here is that it is so wild. They can come out to forage when snows up in the Bob [Marshall Wilderness Area] get so deep. A lot of people have worked to keep it that way."

One target for gas drilling is the 133,000-acre Badger-Two Medicine Roadless Area, which includes the headwaters of two rivers as well as land sacred to the Blackfeet Indians. A remote corner of the Lewis and Clark National Forest, the Badger-Two Medicine is bounded on the west by 2 million acres of national forest wilderness and on the north by Glacier National Park. The Badger-Two Medicine seemed safe in 1997, when National Forest Supervisor Gloria Flora barred new oil and gas leases after ruling that the Front deserved "special attention." Although the ban has not been rescinded, three companies with pre-existing leases now have applied to extract gas there from eight wells.

It is impossible to know how many more wells will follow if the land becomes productive. However, a comparison can be made with the heavily developed mountain-front lands in Alberta. "We've got about 260 wells in an area that covers only a fraction of what is still unspoiled in Montana," Horejsi says.

The fight over the Front boils down to this: Not since James Watt as Interior secretary in the early 1980s was trying to give away public lands as part of the Reagan Revolution has the oil and gas industry had so good a chance to develop even the most sensitive areas of the West. And yet the tradeoff is hardly worthwhile to anyone outside the oil industry. BLM, in an estimate released in 2003, pegged the amount of gas that can be recovered along the Front at 14 billion to 106 billion cubic feet. The United States burns 22 trillion cubic feet of gas yearly. "We're talking about a two-day supply of America's gas from the Badger-Two Medicine," Birkeland says.

Opinion in Montana is running against development. Many local residents work for wildlife and make sacrifices on its behalf. Private efforts to preserve land at the base of the mountains, adjoining Forest Service and BLM holdings, are a major reason that wildlife is either flourishing or recovering. For example, rancher Karl Rappold has put part of his own ranch, which borders the Bob Marshall Wilderness, under conservation easement. The land can never be subdivided and cannot be mined. He works with the advice of a bear biologist, scattering deer and elk carcasses each year when the grizzlies come out of hibernation. "We've learned to respect the bears," says the third-generation rancher, whose family has owned the land since 1876. His concern is that the energy industry has not yet learned that lesson. "The absence of roads is why predators and prey have collected in this particular area," Rappold says. "If you have access roads and pipelines crisscrossing, the grizzly bears are going to have to pack up and move somewhere else—but they have no place to go."

A Kalispell newspaper, *The Daily Inter Lake*, recently cited a 1997 poll in which 60 percent of Montanans objected to oil and gas leasing on the Front. Only 30 percent were in favor, with 10 percent undecided. And the tradeoff for drilling is not good for locals. The newspaper recently concluded that energy development would create only a very few temporary jobs at the expense of land that "is a mecca for hunters and anglers and others."

Mary Sexton, a Teton County commissioner, watched a brief boom in gas exploration in the early 1980s. "Long-term, it was negligible for our economy," she says. Due to changes in how oil and gas development is taxed, the county would get substantially less money if drilling were to resume. "My estimate is what we would get as a county would barely offset what we would have to spend on roads and services," she says. "It would be a wash if there is gas production. If the wells don't produce, it would end up costing us money."

Montana senator Max Baucus has mounted a fight in Congress to keep drilling rigs and gas wells out of the Badger-Two Medicine. His goal is to legislate a three-year moratorium on drilling, during which the Interior Department would be instructed to buy out gas leases or exchange them for leases in less sensitive areas. But the Senate—bowing to Montana's pro-drilling senator, Conrad Burns—refused to include Baucus's modest proposal in a recent energy bill.

Opponents of gas drilling vow they will bow to no one. Chuck Blixrud, owner of the Seven Lazy P and Deep Canyon guest ranches, has lived for 44 years on the north fork of the Teton River, taking hunting and horse parties into the Bob Marshall Wilderness. He has a long memory. In the Watt years of the 1980s, Blixrud traveled the state promoting public protest against oil-industry plans to set off explosions in the 1-million-acre wilderness as part of a seismic exploration scheme. A nationwide upsurge of resistance forced the oilmen—and the Reagan administration—to back off.

Sitting on his porch, recalling past floods and blizzards, Blixrud reflects on how proposed gas drilling would be plunked down right in the middle of choice winter wildlife habitat. "This area, and the Arctic Wildlife Refuge, are two of the wildest places in the United States," he says. "If they are allowed to drill here, it means they will be able to go everywhere."

How Does Our Nation Protect Air Quality?

Federal regulations to protect our air quality date back to the first Air Pollution Control Act of 1955. It was "An Act to provide research and technical assistance relating to air pollution control."[1] This law did little to prevent air pollution, but it did bring national recognition to the dangers pollution posed for public health. It was updated in 1963, and again in 1970, to set more stringent standards for air quality and limits on emissions. In 1990, the Clean Air Act was again amended to address growing concerns about air quality.[2] The issues addressed included air quality standards, motor vehicle standards, motor vehicle emissions, toxic air pollutants, acid rain, and stratospheric ozone depletion.

The Clean Air Act has been successful in several areas. The implementation of the National Ambient Air Quality Standards (NAAQS) has led to decreases in certain harmful emissions: 31% in carbon monoxide, 42% in volatile organic compound (VOC), 37% in sulfur dioxide, 98% in lead, and 37% in particulate matter.[3] Emissions from large industries, diesel particulates, and further reductions in nitrogen and sulfur dioxide still need to be addressed.

The U.S. Environmental Protection Agency (EPA) is developing a set of regulations, the Clean Air Rules of 2004, aimed at continued improvement of our air quality over the next 15 years. The rules address five major areas: interstate air, mercury, non-road diesel emissions, ground-level ozone, and fine particulates. A part of this is New Source Reduction policy, which serves as a good example of the debate that air quality policy can generate. At issue is the possible exemption of old coal-fired plants from clean air standards.[4] It becomes a question of finding economic solutions to protect public health. Whereas one side stresses the economics, opponents view the Clear Skies proposal as "a dramatic example of rolling back protections."[5]

—The Editor

1. American Meteorological Association. *Legislation: A look at U.S. air pollution laws and their amendments*. 1999. Available online at *http://www.ametsoc.org/sloan/cleanair/*.

2. The full text of the Clean Air Act is available online at *http://www.epa.gov/oar/caa/contents.html*.

3. Environmental Defense. *Building on Thirty Years of Success*. 2002.

4. DeWitt, John, and Lee Paddock. "Clean Air and the Politics of Coal." *Issues in Science and Technology*. Winter 2003.

5. Series editor's personal communication with John DeWitt, September 2004.

Clean Air Rules 2004
from the U.S. Environmental Protection Agency

CLEAN AIR RULES OF 2004

The Clean Air Rules are a suite of actions that will dramatically improve America's air quality. Three of the rules specifically address the transport of pollution across state borders (the Interstate Clean Air Rule, Mercury Clean Air Rule and Nonroad Clean Air Rule). These rules provide national tools to achieve significant improvement in air quality and the associated benefits of improved health, longevity and quality of life for all Americans. Taken together, they will make the next 15 years one of the most productive periods of air quality improvement in America's history.

The Clean Air Rules of 2004 encompass the following major rules:

Interstate Air Rule

The Clean Air Interstate Rule (proposed as the Interstate Air Quality Rule) provides states with a solution to the problem of power plant pollution that drifts from one state to another. The rule uses a cap and trade system to reduce the target pollutants by 70%.

Mercury Rule

The Clean Air Mercury Rule (proposed as the Utility Mercury Reductions Rule) will regulate mercury from power plants—the largest domestic source of mercury emissions. This is the first time power-plant mercury emissions will be regulated.

Nonroad Diesel Rule

The Clean Air Nonroad Diesel Rule will change the way diesel engines function to remove emissions and the way diesel fuel is refined to remove sulfur. The black puff of smoke you see coming from construction and other nonroad diesel equipment will be gone forever. The Rule is one of EPA's *Clean Diesel Programs*, which together will result in the most dramatic improvement in air quality since the catalytic converter was first introduced a quarter century ago.

Ozone Rules

The Clean Air Ozone Rules (dealing with 8-hour ground-level ozone designation and implementation) will designate those areas whose air does not meet the health-based standards for ground-level ozone. The ozone rules will classify the seriousness of the problem and require states to submit plans for reducing the levels of ozone in areas where the ozone standards are not met.

Fine Particle Rules

The Clean Air Fine Particle Rules (dealing with PM [particle matter] 2.5 designations and implementation) will designate those areas whose air does not meet the health-based standards for fine-particulate pollution. This will require states to submit plans for reducing the levels of particulate pollution in areas where the fine-particle standards are not met.

The Plain English Guide to the Clean Air Act
from the U.S. Environmental Protection Agency

FEATURES OF THE 1990 CLEAN AIR ACT
The Role of the Federal Government and the Role of the States
Although the 1990 Clean Air Act is a federal law covering the entire country, the states do much of the work to carry out the Act. For example, a state air pollution agency holds a hearing on a permit application by a power or chemical plant or fines a company for violating air pollution limits.

Under this law, EPA sets limits on how much of a pollutant can be in the air anywhere in the United States. This ensures that all Americans have the same basic health and environmental protections. The law allows individual states to have stronger pollution controls, but states are not allowed to have weaker pollution controls than those set for the whole country.

The law recognizes that it makes sense for states to take the lead in carrying out the Clean Air Act, because pollution control problems often require special understanding of local industries, geography, housing patterns, etc.

States have to develop state implementation plans (SIPs) that explain how each state will do its job under the Clean Air Act. A state implementation plan is a collection of the regulations a state will use to clean up polluted areas. The states must involve the public, through hearings and opportunities to comment, in the development of each state implementation plan.

EPA must approve each SIP, and if a SIP isn't acceptable, EPA can take over enforcing the Clean Air Act in that state.

The United States government, through EPA, assists the states by providing scientific research, expert studies, engineering designs and money to support clean air programs.

INTERSTATE AIR POLLUTION
Air pollution often travels from its source in one state to another state. In many metropolitan areas, people live in one state and work or shop in another; air pollution from cars and trucks may spread throughout the interstate area. The

1990 Clean Air Act provides for interstate commissions on air pollution control, which are to develop regional strategies for cleaning up air pollution. The 1990 Clean Air Act includes other provisions to reduce interstate air pollution.

INTERNATIONAL AIR POLLUTION

Air pollution moves across national borders. The 1990 law covers pollution that originates in Mexico and Canada and drifts into the United States and pollution from the United States that reaches Canada and Mexico.

PERMITS

One of the major breakthroughs in the 1990 Clean Air Act is a permit program for larger sources that release pollutants into the air.*

Requiring polluters to apply for a permit is not a new idea. Approximately 35 states have had state-wide permit programs for air pollution. The Clean Water Act requires permits to release pollutants into lakes, rivers or other waterways. Now air pollution is also going to be managed by a national permit system. Under the new program, permits are issued by states or, when a state fails to carry out the Clean Air Act satisfactorily, by EPA. The permit includes information on which pollutants are being released, how much may be released, and what kinds of steps the source's owner or operator is taking to reduce pollution, including plans to monitor (measure) the pollution. The permit system is especially useful for businesses covered by more than one part of the law, since information about all of a source's air pollution will now be in one place. The permit system simplifies and clarifies businesses' obligations for cleaning up air pollution and, over time, can reduce paperwork. For instance, an electric power plant may be covered by the acid rain, hazardous air pollutant and non-attainment (smog) parts of the Clean Air Act; the detailed information required by all these separate sections will be in one place—on the permit.

Permit applications and permits are available to the public; contact your state or regional air pollution control agency or EPA for information on access to these documents.

Businesses seeking permits have to pay permit fees much like car owners paying for car registrations. The money from the fees will help pay for state air pollution control activities.

ENFORCEMENT

The 1990 Clean Air Act gives important new enforcement powers to EPA. It used to be very difficult for EPA to penalize a company for violating the Clean Air Act. EPA has to go to court for even minor violations. The 1990 law enables EPA to fine violators, much like a police officer giving traffic tickets. Other parts of the 1990 law increase penalties for violating the Act and bring the Clean Air Act's enforcement powers in line with other environmental laws.

DEADLINES

The 1990 Clean Air Act sets deadlines for EPA, states, local governments and businesses to reduce air pollution. The deadlines in the 1990 Clean Air Act were designed to be more realistic than deadlines in previous versions of the law, so it is more likely that these deadlines will be met.

PUBLIC PARTICIPATION

Public participation is a very important part of the 1990 Clean Air Act. Throughout the Act, the public is given opportunities to take part in determining how the law will be carried out. For instance, you can take part in hearings on the state and local plans for cleaning up air pollution. You can sue the government or a source's owner or operator to get action when EPA or your state has not enforced the Act. You can request action by the state or EPA against violators.

The reports required by the Act are public documents. A great deal of information will be collected on just how much pollution is being released; these monitoring (measuring) data will be available to the public. The 1990 Clean Air Act ordered EPA to set up clearinghouses to collect and give out technical information. Typically, these clearinghouses will serve the public as well as state and other air pollution control agencies. . . .

MARKET APPROACHES FOR REDUCING AIR POLLUTION; ECONOMIC INCENTIVES

The 1990 Clean Air Act has many features designed to clean up air pollution as efficiently and inexpensively as possible, letting businesses make choices on the best way to reach pollution cleanup goals. These new flexible programs are called market or market-based approaches. For instance, the acid rain cleanup program offers businesses choices as to how they reach their pollution reduction goals and includes pollution allowances that can be traded, bought and sold.

The 1990 Clean Air Act provides economic incentives for cleaning up pollution. For instance, gasoline refiners can get credits if they produce cleaner gasoline than required, and they can use those credits when their gasoline doesn't quite meet cleanup requirements.

ENDNOTES

* A source can be a power plant, factory or anything that releases pollutants into the air. Cars, trucks and other motor vehicles are sources, and consumer products and machines used in industry can be sources too. Sources that stay in one place are referred to as stationary sources; sources that move around, like cars or planes, are called mobile sources.

What Is the Clean Water Act?

There are several water policy issues that probably made it possible for you to take a clean shower today. Water policies address questions such as water quality (Is the water clean?) and water quantity (Is there enough?). In 1972, the U.S. Environmental Protection Agency (EPA) passed the Clean Water Act (CWA) "to restore and maintain the chemical, physical, and biological integrity of the Nation's Waters."[1] The law set ambitious goals for treating municipal and industrial wastewater, expanding federal policies to be enforced by the states, providing federal assistance for treatment plant construction, and protecting wetlands. However, groundwater and the amount of water used is not regulated by the CWA.

The following EPA information offers an introduction to the CWA. Over 30 years after the CWA was passed, the job of protecting our nation's surface waters is still not done. According to an August 2004 EPA press release, further control of sewer overflows is vital to reducing risks to public health and protecting the environment.[2] The EPA found that in 31 states and the District of Columbia, 772 combined sewer systems still discharge about 850 billion gallons of untreated wastewater and stormwater each year.[3] States report that nonpoint source pollution is still the largest source of water pollution.[4] Nonpoint pollution includes many contaminants (fertilizers, oil, sediment, salts, pesticides) transported by rain and snow. In 1987, the CWA was amended to include section 319, the Nonpoint Source Management Program, which offers financial and technical assistance to states for dealing with nonpoint pollution.

Science has shown us that wetlands are important for maintaining good water quality. Included in the CWA is a section that protects 50% of the United States' remaining wetlands.[5] Section 404 deals with physical alteration (filling or dredging) of wetlands. Of current concern to many who understand the value of wetlands is the government's "guidance memo" to wetland regulators that puts 20 million acres of wetlands and small streams in danger of pollution and degradation from development.[6]

—The Editor

1. Federal Water Pollution Control Act (As Amended Through P. L. 107-303), November 27, 2002. Available online at *http://www.epa.gov/region5/water/pdf/ecwa.pdf*.

2. U.S. Environmental Protection Agency Press Release. *Despite Progress, Sewer Overflows Still Pose Health and Environmental Concerns*. August 26, 2004. Available online at *http://www.epa.gov/newsroom/*.

3. Ibid.

4. U.S. Environmental Protection Agency. Factsheet. *Threats to Wetlands*. Available online at *http://www.epa.gov/owow/wetlands/facts/threats.pdf*.

5. U.S. Environmental Protection Agency. Factsheet. *What Is Nonpoint Source Pollution?* Available online at *http://www.epa.gov/owow/nps/qa.html*.

6. Nickens, T. Edward. "Small Is Beautiful." *National Wildlife Federation*. June–July 2004.

Introduction to the Clean Water Act
from the U.S. Environmental Protection Agency

The Clean Water Act (CWA) is the cornerstone of surface water quality protection in the United States. (The Act does not deal directly with ground water nor with water quantity issues.) The statute employs a variety of regulatory and non-regulatory tools to sharply reduce direct pollutant discharges into waterways, finance municipal wastewater treatment facilities, and manage polluted runoff. These tools are employed to achieve the broader goal of restoring and maintaining the chemical, physical, and biological integrity of the nation's waters so that they can support "the protection and propagation of fish, shellfish, and wildlife and recreation in and on the water."

For many years following the passage of CWA in 1972, EPA, states, and Indian tribes focused mainly on the chemical aspects of the "integrity" goal. During the last decade, however, more attention has been given to physical and biological integrity. Also, in the early decades of the Act's implementation, efforts focused on regulating discharges from traditional "point source" facilities, such as municipal sewage plants and industrial facilities, with little attention paid to runoff from streets, construction sites, farms, and other "wet-weather" sources.

Starting in the late 1980s, efforts to address polluted runoff have increased significantly. For "nonpoint" runoff, voluntary programs, including cost-sharing with landowners are the key tool. For "wet weather point sources" like urban storm sewer systems and construction sites, a regulatory approach is being employed.

Evolution of CWA programs over the last decade has also included something of a shift from a program-by-program, source-by-source, pollutant-by-pollutant approach to more holistic watershed-based strategies. Under the watershed approach equal emphasis is placed on protecting healthy waters and restoring impaired ones. A full array of issues are addressed, not just those subject to CWA regulatory authority. Involvement of stakeholder groups in the development and implementation of strategies for achieving and maintaining state water quality and other environmental goals is another hallmark of this approach.

CLEAN WATER ACT HISTORY

Growing public awareness and concern for controlling water pollution led to enactment of the Federal Water Pollution Control Act Amendments of 1972. As amended in 1977, this law became commonly known as the Clean Water Act. The Act established the basic structure for regulating discharges of pollutants into the waters of the United States. It gave EPA the authority to implement pollution control programs such as setting wastewater standards for industry. The Clean Water Act also continued requirements to set water quality standards for all contaminants in surface waters. The Act made it unlawful for any person to discharge any pollutant from a point source into navigable waters, unless a permit was obtained under its provisions. It also funded the construction of sewage treatment plants under the construction grants program and recognized the need for planning to address the critical problems posed by nonpoint source pollution.

Subsequent enactments modified some of the earlier Clean Water Act provisions. Revisions in 1981 streamlined the municipal construction grants process, improving the capabilities of treatment plants built under the program. Changes in 1987 phased out the construction grants program, replacing it with the State Water Pollution Control Revolving Fund, more commonly known as the Clean Water State Revolving Fund. This new funding strategy addressed water quality needs by building on EPA-State partnerships.

Over the years, many other laws have changed parts of the Clean Water Act. Title I of the Great Lakes Critical Programs Act of 1990, for example, put into place parts of the Great Lakes Water Quality Agreement of 1978, signed by the U.S. and Canada, where the two nations agreed to reduce certain toxic pollutants in the Great Lakes. That law required EPA to establish water quality criteria for the Great Lakes addressing 29 toxic pollutants with maximum levels that are safe for humans, wildlife, and aquatic life. It also required EPA to help the States implement the criteria on a specific schedule.

What Are Our Nation's Policies for Water Use?

In their 2003 book, *Rivers of Life*, Sandra Postel, director of the Global Water Policy Project, and Brian Richter, director of The Nature Conservancy's Freshwater Initiative, discuss the future of rivers in the United States. Having observed the rates at which certain plants and animals are becoming endangered, the decline of fisheries, and the drying of rivers from overpumping, Postel and Richter caution that changes in river management policy are needed.

The following excerpts highlight the issues. The question of who gets to use the water is one that becomes more and more important as the U.S. population grows and needs more water to carry out daily activities. Long-standing laws and policies regulating water use are not based on scientific understandings of the connection between surface water and groundwater.

For example, a 1904 Texas court decision was based on the assumption that groundwater movement was "secret and occult," and said that regulation would be impossible. Therefore, Texas, like many western states, adopted the English "rule of capture," which means if you can pump it, you can take it.[1] Although this law has been challenged, it remains in effect today. Water rights laws in many eastern states are "riparian laws," meaning that people can use the water, but do not own the rights to it. Many water use laws today favor economic development, with little regard to maintaining the health of the river ecosystem.

Postel and Richter cite a host of existing government policies that could be used to restore and regulate the flow of U.S. rivers. They identify the Clean Water Act (CWA), whose goal is "to restore and maintain the chemical, physical, and biological integrity of the Nation's waters," as the most powerful existing tool. Historically, the CWA has mainly focused on the chemical aspects of river water.

The authors ask, "Do rivers and the life within them have a right to water?" The answer, according to most legal systems today, is no. Science continually gives us more knowledge about how to maintain the health of rivers, about the connections between surface water and groundwater, and about how the health of rivers affects all of us. It is time, the authors declare, to develop and implement a basic code of ethics in river policy by using the policy tools that already exist.

—The Editor

1. Glennon, Robert. *Water Follies*. Washington, D.C.: Island Press, 2002, pp. 89–90.

Rivers for Life
by Sandra Postel and Brian Richter

THE POLICY TOOLBOX

At a gathering in London in November 2000, former South African president Nelson Mandela captured the essence of the new challenge ahead for societies in their relationships with rivers. The occasion was the release of the final report of the World Commission on Dams, the first-ever independent global review of the effectiveness of large dams in promoting sustainable human development. "It is one thing to find fault with an existing system," Mandela said. "It is another thing altogether, a more difficult task, to replace it with an approach that is better." Surely no one knows this better than Nelson Mandela.

Society's existing approach to managing rivers clearly is not working. Numerous indicators—from the rates of species imperilment, to the decline of fisheries, to the drying up of river flows—show that rivers are at risk. Now that scientists have devised methods of determining how much water a river needs, society is confronted with a clear call to action: will we ensure that those water needs are met?

Many of the conflicts over water use and management that have erupted in recent years reflect the mounting tension between those who wish to heed this call to action and those vested in protecting the status quo. Within the United States, disputes have broken out in recent years over water allocations between "offstream" uses of rivers (e.g., irrigation) and "instream" uses (e.g., protection of endangered species) in the Klamath River basin of California and Oregon; the Snake River basin of Idaho; the Truckee-Carson river system of Nevada; the Apalachicola-Chattahoochee-Flint river basin of Georgia, Alabama, and Florida; and the Shepaug River system of Connecticut—to name just a few. Similar conflicts are arising around the world in river basins large and small, from Southeast Asia's Mekong to South America's Paraguay to southern Africa's Okavango.

Striking a more optimal balance between human water uses and those of rivers themselves will require adjustments. But they need not be wrenching ones, and in the end they will produce a more lasting set of benefits from rivers. A significant portion of society is coming to understand more deeply that human welfare is tightly hitched to the health of the ecosystems around us—that protecting rivers also protects ourselves. Moreover, there is no single, static optimum allocation of water between people and nature. Just as our scientific understanding is evolving about how much water a river needs to be healthy and well-functioning, so is our collective sense about the levels of protection rivers need to be given.

It is now clear, however, that securing the freshwater flows needed to conserve biodiversity and safeguard critical ecosystem services will require governments to reshape laws and policies that were crafted in an earlier time—one concerned with controlling rivers for economic advancement, not with protecting their ecological health for this and future generations. Recasting the rules of river use and management will not be easy. But it is necessary. As Thomas Jefferson wisely observed in 1786, "laws and institutions must go hand in hand with the progress of the human mind." . . .

U.S. POLICY LACKS FOCUS ON ECOLOGICAL HEALTH

With each passing year, the need for greater protection of river flows in the United States becomes more apparent. Two centuries of dam building, levee construction, and straightening of river channels have left very few river segments in anything close to their natural state: only 2 percent of U.S. rivers and streams remain free-flowing. Conflicts over the allocation of water between human needs and ecosystem needs have been intensifying across the country, from west to east and north to south. Freshwater life in running waters is increasingly at risk.

Many western U.S. rivers are oversubscribed, leaving little or no flow to meet ecosystem requirements. Similar signs of stress are apparent now in the eastern portions of the country, areas long thought immune to the water predicaments of the naturally drier West. Nearly 500 kilometers of Vermont's rivers are impaired due to flow alterations and heavy withdrawals. The Ipswich River in Massachusetts now periodically runs dry during the summer months because heavy groundwater pumping for suburban lawn irrigation is depleting the river's base flows. Excessive water withdrawals and diversions have impaired the flow of numerous Connecticut rivers, including the Shepaug, the subject of a citizens suit brought before the state's Supreme Court. In the rapidly growing Southeast, Georgia, Alabama, and Florida have haggled for more than a decade over sharing the waters of the Apalachicola-Chattahoochee-Flint river basin, an ecosystem seriously threatened by rapidly increasing water extractions and flow modifications.

Despite widespread degradation of its river systems, the United States has no overarching vision or goal to secure the flows that rivers need to support the diversity of freshwater life and to sustain ecological functions. Historically, the U.S. government has deferred to the states in matters of water allocation, use, and management. This acquiescence, however, is a matter of choice. The U.S. Constitution makes clear that when state law conflicts with federal, the latter trumps the former. In the area of water allocation, this notion was upheld in the landmark 1899 decision in *United States* v. *Rio Grande Irrigation Co.*, which effectively subordinated state-authorized water uses to federal powers over commerce and public land. According to University of Colorado water-law scholar David Getches, early cases also made it clear that federal preemption of state water law did not require any special legislative action.

In practice, however, federal authorities have rarely interfered with state systems of water rights and allocation, and so the states have called most of the shots. Each state has a body of water law that derives from its constitution, legislative acts, and court decisions. The eastern and western states abide by different legal doctrines, which reflect in part their dissimilar climatic, historical, and economic circumstances. Most eastern states apply the "riparian" doctrine of water law, according to which parties adjacent to rivers and streams can make reasonable use of those waters. Under the riparian system, individuals do not own rights to water. The state permits the use of water bodies, often accompanied by conditions or requirements that ensure such uses do not cause unreasonable harm to others.

By contrast, most western states abide by the "prior appropriation" doctrine, often encapsulated by the motto "first in time, first in right." Those who made the earliest claims on a river have the highest priority rights to its water. Once granted, water rights become the private property of their holder. These rights are what lawyers call "usufructory" rights: they are rights to use water, not to own it outright—hence the other motto that has characterized western water law, "use it or lose it." Along with a specified volume, each water right comes with a date that determines its ranking in the allocation hierarchy. In times of drought, the holder of a more senior water right—one with an earlier date—will get all of his or her water before a more junior rights holder gets any. State agencies administer the applications for and granting of water rights, and any legal challenges are typically handled by state courts.

Federal authorities over rivers take place within the context of these state legal systems. These include federal laws, such as the National Environmental Policy Act (1969), the Clean Water Act (1972), and the Endangered Species Act (1973); case law derived from federal court decisions; as well as authorities granted under the U.S. Constitution, such as the commerce, property, and supremacy clauses. These overlapping and at times competing federal and state authorities would almost certainly not be the policy framework of choice for water management today if, like South Africa, the United States had the opportunity to start over with a blank slate. But it is the system that is in place, and so the challenge lies in interpreting, enforcing, and where necessary, amending these authorities such that they collectively do a better job of balancing human uses of water with the protection of aquatic ecosystems. Our review of the relevant federal and state laws and policies shows a great deal of potential for the protection and restoration of river flows, but most of it so far is unrealized.

FEDERAL OPTIONS

At the federal level, there are at least nine categories of actions or measures that agencies could take to improve river flows. Each of these measures has succeeded in preserving or restoring flows in some cases—establishing all as viable policy tools— but none has been applied broadly enough to significantly improve river flows on a wide scale. Although existing laws and powers seem to give federal agencies the authority to limit flow modifications in order to safeguard river health, this action has not been taken.

The most powerful federal authorities over river flows derive from the commerce clause (Article 1, Section 8) of the U.S. Constitution and the Clean Water Act of 1972. Under the commerce clause, the federal government has the power to regulate commerce among the states and with other nations. Because waters may be used for commercial navigation, it gives Congress some authority over water management. Initially, this authority was interpreted narrowly to cover only activities causing an obstruction to navigable waters. Over time, however, federal courts expanded the definition of "navigable" and the range of activities to which the commerce clause applied. As David Gillilan and Thomas Brown write in their analysis of instream flow protection measures in the western United States, "Eventually the courts determined that rivers did not actually have to be navigable for the Congress to assert its commerce powers. By the time Congress passed the Clean Water Act in 1972, the courts had allowed the federal

Federal Authorities for Protecting River Flows in the United States

ACTION OR MEASURE

➤ Revising management of federal dams built for irrigation, flood control, water supply, hydropower, and navigation

➤ Licensing nonfederal hydropower dams

➤ Listing freshwater species as endangered

➤ Protecting habitat for species listed as endangered

➤ Gaining federal "reserved" water rights through state legal systems

➤ Establishing federal "nonreserved" water rights

➤ Protecting water quality and overall river health

➤ Designating rivers as "wild and scenic"

➤ Controlling activities on public lands that would impact streamflows

PRINCIPAL AGENTS

➤ Army Corps of Engineers

➤ Bureau of Reclamation

government to assert jurisdiction over all the waters of the United States, including rivers, lakes, streams, estuaries, and even wetlands."

The federal Clean Water Act (CWA) offers the broadest and clearest mandate to the U.S. Congress to protect river health. Coupled with powers granted under the commerce

> Department of Energy

> Tennessee Valley Authority

> Bonneville Power Administration

> Western Area Power Administration

> Federal Energy Regulatory Commission

> Fish and Wildlife Service

> Marine Fisheries Service (for salmon)

> Secretary of the Interior

> All federal agencies impacting rivers

> National Park Service

> Forest Service

> Bureau of Land Management

> Indian tribes

> Environmental Protection Agency

> National Park Service

> U.S. Congress

clause, it leaves little doubt that the federal government has all the authority it needs to protect and restore the flow of rivers. The expressed goal of the act is "to restore and maintain the chemical, physical, and biological integrity of the Nation's waters." During three decades of implementing the act, however, Congress and the federal agencies administering it have focused primarily on protecting chemical integrity through the setting of water quality standards, pollution control requirements, and best management practices. They have done little explicitly to regulate the quantity and timing of river flows to protect the physical and biological integrity of rivers.

Several events and court decisions during the 1990s extended the reach of the CWA to river flows. So far, however, these have been relatively isolated cases that demonstrate the act's potential potency but that have so far not led to broader protections. . . .

POWER TOOLS FOR THE STATES

With states effectively having primary responsibility for water allocation and management, they have considerable leverage to secure environmental flows for rivers. As with federal authorities, however, the application of state powers has been patchy, inconsistent, and so far mostly ineffective at protecting the ecological integrity of rivers. Many state efforts still focus on establishing minimum flow requirements, which may keep water running in rivers but not necessarily at the volumes or times that the ecosystems need. Many are also oriented toward safeguarding flows for anglers, boaters, and other recreationists, but not for the ecosystem itself.

A number of policy tools for restoring healthy flows to rivers are available to the states. Although their applicability and practicality vary from state to state, these options include legislating the establishment of environmental flows for rivers, using permit programs to enforce basin-wide limits on flow modifications, granting or transferring water rights for instream purposes, setting conservation goals and requiring conservation programs, and, as legal cases arise, applying judicial protections, such as the public trust doctrine.

The ability most states have to grant, deny, and set conditions on permissions to extract water from state water bodies (often surface water and groundwater) gives them substantial potential to protect river flows. To be used effectively, however, state permitting programs need to be directly keyed to the maintenance of ecological flow regimes such that the sum of all flow modifications in a river do not exceed the threshold defined for that place and time. A "percent-of-flow approach" used by the Southwest Florida Water Management District comes close to this idea. In 1989, the District, which is one of five such geographic districts responsible for managing Florida waters, began limiting direct withdrawals from unimpounded rivers to a percentage of streamflow at the time of withdrawal. For example, cumulative withdrawals from the Peace and Alafia rivers are limited to 10 percent of the daily flow; during periods of very low flow, withdrawals are prohibited completely. The District is now considering using percentage withdrawal limits that vary among seasons and flow ranges in order to better protect the ecological health of rivers under its jurisdiction.

Importantly, this mechanism preserves the natural flow regime of rivers by linking water withdrawals to a percentage of flow—specifically, by ensuring that a major percentage of the natural flow is protected every day. If a new permit application would cause total withdrawals to exceed the threshold, denial of the permit is recommended unless the applicant can demonstrate that the additional withdrawals will not cause adverse ecological impacts. This provision allows for flexibility, but places the burden of proof on potential water users to show that their withdrawals would not harm the ecosystem.

A number of New England states have also taken some positive steps in recent years. In July 2000, Vermont revised its water standards to recognize the need to adjust human-induced flow alterations in order to protect aquatic habitat. The New England office of the U.S. Environmental Protection

Agency is working hand in hand with states in the region to encourage the adoption of standards more protective of environmental flows. It has also funded the Connecticut River Joint Commission to examine ways to improve policies affecting flows in the upper Connecticut, New England's largest river.

In western states that apply the doctrine of prior appropriation, the challenge is to establish instream water rights that are sufficient to sustain ecological flows for rivers. None have done this adequately, but many have taken steps either to reserve a portion of flows for instream purposes or, more commonly, to establish minimum streamflows, although these are usually geared toward protecting certain fish species rather than whole ecosystems. Perhaps more importantly, all the western states have criteria for evaluating requests for new appropriative water rights and changes to existing ones, and nearly all (Colorado and Oklahoma are the exceptions) require that new appropriations serve the public interest. Early on, the public interest tended to be equated with economic development, but increasingly public interest criteria are being used to protect river flows from further depletion or modification.

As a result, water rights dedicated to ecosystem protection can now often enjoy the same legal status as rights used for irrigation or other extractive purposes. A major drawback to instream flow water rights designations, however, is that they often have such a low priority date that they do not offer much protection to rivers. To rectify this, some states allocate funds for the purchase of existing higher-priority water rights and then convert them to instream rights. Another important limitation of instream water rights is that they are usually quantified as constant year-round or monthly values that do not come close to approximating a river's naturally variable pattern of flow; they therefore often do little to protect or restore ecosystem health.

One intriguing idea proposed in recent years is that of turning these conventional instream water rights upside down. Instead of prescribing flows for ecosystem support, and implicitly allocating all remaining flows for extractive or other economic purposes, so-called "upside-down instream flow water rights" are defined by turning the question around and asking instead: how much can a river's natural flow pattern be modified in order to meet irrigation, hydropower, and other water development demands and yet still meet the flow needs of the river ecosystem itself? This degree of water development is then specified, and all the remaining flows are allocated to protection of ecosystem functions and services. Attorneys Nicole Silk and Robert Wigington of The Nature Conservancy, along with Jack McDonald of the Northwestern School of Law at Lewis and Clark College, make a strong case for legal recognition of upside-down instream flow water rights either as federally reserved water rights in relation to national parks, forests, or other public lands; or as appropriative rights under state law. These rights may be most applicable, they note, on rivers not overly developed and may work best when implemented with a precautionary approach: that is, reserve only a modest amount of water for development initially, and add more incrementally as scientists develop clearer delineations of where ecological harm will occur.

In essence, upside-down instream flow water rights are a way of implementing the shift toward ecologically compatible water development within the context of the appropriative water rights system in the western United States. In many ways it is similar to the "benchmarking methodology" being applied in parts of Australia. The idea is to permit the withdrawal or modification of only as much flow as the best available scientific evidence can support as unharmful to the river's health. If that threshold is exceeded, then at least society is aware that some degree of ecosystem health is being sacrificed for more water development.

Another underused tool available to the states to protect river flows is their authority (under Section 401 of the federal Clean Water Act) to certify water projects for compliance with state water quality requirements. This authority applies to projects that require a federal license or permit, including hydropower licenses issued by FERC [Federal Energy Regulatory Commission] as well as permits issued by the Army Corps of Engineers for dredging, filling, or altering watercourses or wetlands (under Section 404 of the CWA). Recent court rulings have made clear that states can use this certification authority to powerful effect. In a key 1994 decision (PUD No. 1 of *Jefferson County* v. *Washington Department of Ecology*), the U.S. Supreme Court held that a state could impose flow conditions on a FERC-licensed project if necessary to protect the state's designated uses of the river. The Court swept away any notion that the CWA applies only to water quality and not to water quantity, stating that this is "an artificial distinction," since in many cases "a sufficient lowering of the water quantity in a body of water could destroy all of its designated uses. . . ." The Court said the state of Washington was permitted to set flow requirements in its certification of a hydroelectric facility on the Dosewallips River, because the flows were needed to maintain the designated uses the state had established for the river. . . .

ETHICS IN RIVER POLICY

Do rivers and the life within them have a right to water? In most modern-day legal systems, the answer is no. Water is typically the property of the state, and rights to it are conferred by governments to individuals, cities, corporations, and other human enterprises. Allocations for fish, mussels, and rivers themselves are made only if agents of government deem such allocations socially beneficial, or necessary to fulfill any trust obligations that may exist.

The ethical dimensions of society's water use and management choices could conveniently be ignored as long as those choices did not kill other living things. With freshwater life being extinguished at record rates, however, this is clearly not the case today. Our water management decisions have serious ethical implications, and yet these rarely enter the debate over water plans, projects, and allocations. This may not be surprising given that governments have failed even to provide safe drinking water to all people, which results in several million human deaths each year. Yet our moral obligations both to our fellow human beings and to other life-forms implore us to begin injecting these other ethical implications into our policy choices—to manage water as the basis of life for all living things, rather than as a commodity for the benefit of some.

The fact that rivers have no right to water, and that portions of them maybe held as private property fits into an ethical code grounded in prevailing socioeconomic philosophies, but one that is neither universal nor unchanging. The American conservationist Aldo Leopold viewed the extension of ethics to the natural environment as "an evolutionary possibility and an ecological necessity." More recently, Harvard biologist Edward O. Wilson notes in his book *Consilience* that, historically, ethical codes have arisen through the interplay of biology and culture. "Ethics, in the empiricist view," Wilson observes, "is conduct favored consistently enough throughout a society to be expressed as a code of principles."

In a practical sense, an ethic serves as a guide to right conduct in the face of complex decisions we do not fully understand but that may have serious consequences. Scientists are making clear that the health and life of rivers depend upon a naturally variable flow pattern. As scientists and economists quantify more of the ecosystem services at risk, societies will come to see that the protection of ecosystems is not only an ethical action, but a rational one: acts of stewardship and economic self-interest will converge. But rates of species extinctions and ecosystem decline are too rapid to wait for this convergence to take place. We need some ethical precepts to guide us wisely through this time of risk and uncertainty, and toward actions that preserve rather than foreclose options for this and future generations.

The principle of the public trust offers a good foundation for a code of water ethics in the twenty-first century. Making it a practical guide, however, requires some pragmatic rules and tools. An important one is the ecosystem support allocation, which we have already described in some detail.

Another is the precautionary principle, which essentially says that given the rapid pace of ecosystem decline, the irreversible nature of many of the resulting losses, and the high value of freshwater ecosystem services to human societies, it is wise to err on the side of protecting too much rather than too little of the freshwater habitat that remains. It operates like an insurance policy: we buy extra protection in the face of uncertainty.

Applying the precautionary principle to the protection of river health would mean dedicating a large enough share of natural river flows to ecosystem support to accommodate scientific uncertainty over how much water the river system needs. The Benchmarking Methodology that scientists are using to set environmental flow requirements for rivers in Queensland, Australia, takes a precautionary approach by identifying the levels of flow modification beyond which there is increased risk of unacceptable ecological damage. Under Hawaii's new water policies, the state must apply the precautionary principle as a guide for allocating water in fulfillment of its public trust obligations. And in what is perhaps the strongest recognition of the precautionary principle by an international water institution, the International Joint Commission (IJC) adopted it as a guiding principle for protecting the Great Lakes, which straddle Canada and the United States. In a 1999 report to both governments, the IJC cites the precautionary approach as one of five principles, noting: "Because there is uncertainty about the availability of Great Lakes water in the future— . . . and uncertainty about the extent to which removals and consumptive use harm, perhaps irreparably, the integrity of the Basin ecosystem— caution should be used in managing water to protect the resource for the future. There should be a bias in favor of retaining water in the system and using it more efficiently and effectively."

New scientific knowledge about the importance of healthy rivers and the flows required to sustain them has placed upon us new responsibilities. The establishment of ecosystem flow reserves for rivers is essential to protect the diversity of life and to preserve options for future generations. The scientific, legal, policy, and economic tools exist to make these reserves a reality. A basic code of ethics requires that we act.

Why Is the Pumping of Groundwater an Issue?

Groundwater is the water that fills the spaces between soil or rocks under the ground surface. Large deposits of groundwater are called aquifers. A major difference between surface water and groundwater is that you can see one and not the other. Another major difference is that groundwater refills, or recharges, much more slowly than do rivers or lakes.[1] However, there is a very important point of connection. Surface water and groundwater are not separate. Depending on the lay of the land or the time of year, rivers can recharge groundwater, and groundwater can feed streams or wetlands.

As the following article explains, groundwater is a major concern in the United States because of huge increases in pumping groundwater for drinking, for industry, and for irrigation of crops. A first concern is that we will deplete our groundwater supplies. For example, more water is being pumped from the Ogallala Aquifer, which runs through seven states from Texas to South Dakota, than is being recharged. A second concern is that, as we pump groundwater, we are also sucking water out of our rivers and wetlands.

The laws regulating groundwater pumping place no restrictions on the amount that can be taken, allowing pumping for "reasonable use." Author Robert Glennon, a professor at the University of Arizona, outlines the many problems with such an unregulated use of our nation's groundwater. Issues include the cost of pumping, the quality of the water, the dangers of land sinking after water withdrawals, and the impact on surface waters and wetlands. As an example, the author shows that in Arizona, groundwater pumping has "dried up or degraded 90 percent of the state's once perennial desert streams, rivers, and riparian habitats." He points out that state government rules and regulations should be used to reform our current policies. Needed reforms include implementing water conservation programs, establishing minimum stream flow levels, and prohibiting drilling of new wells in areas connected to surface water.

Robert Glennon is Morris K. Udall Professor of Law and Public Policy at the University of Arizona. He is the author of *Water Follies: Groundwater Pumping and the Fate of America's Fresh Waters* (Island Press, 2002).

—The Editor

1. Freeze, R. Allan, and John A. Cherry. *Groundwater.* Englewood Cliffs, NJ: Prentice-Hall, Inc., 1979, p. 5.

The Perils of Groundwater Pumping
by Robert Glennon

The excessive "mining" of our aquifers is causing environmental degradation on a potentially enormous scale.

The next time you reach for a bottle of spring water, consider that it may have come from a well that is drying up a blue-ribbon trout stream. The next time you dine at McDonald's, note that the fries are all the same length. That's because the farmers who grow the potatoes irrigate their fields, perhaps with groundwater from wells adjacent to nearby rivers. The next time you purchase gold jewelry, consider that it may have come from a mine that has pumped so much groundwater to be able to work the gold-bearing rock that 60 to 100 years will pass before the water table recovers. The next time you water your suburban lawn, pause to reflect on what that is doing to the nearby wetland. And the next time you visit Las Vegas and flip on the light in your hotel room, consider that the electricity may have come from a coal-fired power plant supplied by a slurry pipeline that uses groundwater critical to springs sacred to the Hopi people.

These and countless other seemingly innocuous activities reflect our individual and societal dependence on groundwater. From Tucson to Tampa Bay, from California's Central Valley to Down East Maine, rivers and lakes have disappeared, and fresh water is becoming scarce. Groundwater pumping—for domestic consumption, irrigation, or mining—causes bodies of water and wetlands to dry up; the ground beneath us to collapse; and fish, wildlife, and trees to die. The excessive pumping of our aquifers has created an environmental catastrophe known to relatively few scientists and water management experts and to those who are unfortunate enough to have suffered the direct consequences. This phenomenon is occurring not just in the arid West with its tradition of battling over water rights, but even in places we think of as relatively wet.

As a country, we have dramatically increased our reliance on groundwater. This increase has dried up rivers and lakes, because there is a hydrologic connection between groundwater and surface water. Yet the legal rules governing water use usually ignore this link. This disconnection between law and science is a major cause of the problem. So too is our refusal to recognize the unsustainability of our water use. Significant reform is necessary if we are to prevent further degradation of our rivers, streams, lakes, wetlands, and estuaries.

GROUNDWATER USE AND CONSEQUENCES

Groundwater pumping in the United States has increased dramatically in the past few decades. For domestic purposes alone, groundwater use jumped from 2.9 trillion gallons in 1965 to about 6.8 trillion gallons in 1995, or 24,000 gallons for every man, woman, and child. But domestic consumption is only a small fraction of the country's total groundwater use, which totaled almost 28 trillion gallons in 1995. Farmers used two-thirds of that to irrigate crops; the mining industry, especially for copper, coal, and gold production, pumped about 770 billion gallons. Groundwater constitutes more than 25 percent of the nation's water supply. In 1995, California alone pumped 14,500 billion gallons of groundwater per day. Groundwater withdrawals actually exceeded surface water diversions in Florida, Kansas, Nebraska, and Mississippi. In the United States, more than half of the population relies on groundwater for their drinking water supply. Groundwater pumping has become a global problem because 1.5 billion people (one-quarter of the world's population) depend on groundwater for drinking water.

Groundwater is an extraordinarily attractive source of water for farms, mines, cities, and homeowners because it is available throughout the year and it exists almost everywhere in the country. During the various ice ages, much of the country was covered with huge freshwater lakes. Water from these lakes percolated into the ground and collected in aquifers. Unlike rivers and streams, which are few and far between, especially in the West, aquifers exist below almost the entire country.

The legal system has fostered our increasing use of groundwater by developing two sets of rules for allocating rights to divert water from rivers and lakes. In the East, the riparian system allows owners of property on rivers or lakes to divert water for a variety of purposes. In the West, the prior appropriation doctrine—the essence of which is "first-in-time, first-in-right"—gives superior rights to the earliest diverters. However, the legal system developed a completely different set of rules for controlling groundwater use. When U.S. courts developed groundwater law in the 19th century, hydrology was an infant science. In 1850, the Supreme Court of Connecticut explained that the movement of water beneath the surface of the earth moved according to principles that could not be known or regulated. "These influences are so secret, changeable, and uncontrollable, we cannot subject them to the regulations of law, nor build upon them a system of rules, as has been done with streams upon the surface," the court said. This reasoning made sense in 1850; since then, however, the law in most states has not kept pace with advances in the science of hydrology. As a consequence, the legal rules have failed to conform with physical reality. Principles of either riparianism or prior appropriation govern surface water, whereas the "reasonable use" doctrine governs groundwater pumping. Under this doctrine, an owner of land may pump as much water as he or she desires so long as it is for a "reasonable use," which is essentially no restriction whatsoever.

Overdrafting or "mining" groundwater creates serious problems. Because water is heavy, about two pounds per quart, more energy is needed to lift water from lower levels. The costs of this energy may be substantial: In Arizona, the electric energy to run a commercial irrigation well may cost $2,000 per month. The drilling of new and deeper wells may be required, which is often a considerable expense. Pumping from lower levels may produce poorer quality water because naturally occurring elements, such as arsenic, fluoride, and radon, are more prevalent at deeper levels in the earth, and the earth's higher internal temperature at these levels dissolves more of these elements into solution. As the water deteriorates in quality, it may violate U.S. Environmental Protection Agency regulations, requiring either that the water be subject to expensive treatment processes or that the well be turned off, thus eliminating that source of water. Along coastal areas, over-drafting may cause the intrusion of saltwater into the aquifer, rendering the water no longer potable. This problem is quite serious in California, Florida, Texas, and South Carolina. Another consequence of overdrafting is the prospect of land subsidence, in which the land's surface actually cracks or drops, in some cases dramatically. In California's San Joaquin Valley, the land surface dropped between 25 and 30 feet between 1925 and 1977. Land subsidence has damaged homes and commer-cial structures and reduced property values. Pumping north of Tampa Bay in Pasco County has cracked the foundations, walls, and ceilings of local residents' homes, resulting in lawsuits, insurance claims, and considerable ill will.

A final consequence of groundwater pumping is its impact on surface water, including lakes, ponds, rivers, creeks, streams, springs, wetlands, and estuaries. These consequences range from minimal to catastrophic. An example of the latter is the Santa Cruz River in Tucson. Once a verdant riparian system with a lush canopy provided by cottonwood and willow trees, groundwater pumping has lowered the water table, drained the river of its flow, killed the cottonwood and willow trees, and driven away the local wildlife. The river has become an oxymoron—a dry river—a pathetic desiccated sandbox.

HOW DOES A RIVER GO DRY?

Fueled by the energy of the sun and the force of gravity, water continually moves through a succession of different phases, called the hydrologic cycle. The sun's energy evaporates seawater from the oceans' surface, leaving behind the salts and circulating the water into the atmosphere. After wind currents carry the moisture-laden air over land, the increase in relative humidity eventually causes the water to condense and produces precipitation. When the water falls to earth, some of it immediately evaporates into the sky, another portion runs off the land to creeks, streams, and rivers, and some infiltrates the ground, in a process known as recharge. A portion of the groundwater near rivers and streams eventually emerges from the ground, in a process called discharge, to augment the surface flows of rivers or streams. Groundwater pumping essentially interrupts this cycle by removing water, directly or indirectly, that would otherwise discharge from aquifers to rivers, streams, and other surface water bodies.

Groundwater and surface water are not separate categories of water any more than liquid water and ice are truly separate. The designations groundwater and surface water merely describe the physical location of the water in the hydrologic cycle. Indeed, groundwater and surface water form a continuum. In some regions of the country, virtually all groundwater was once stream flow that seeped into the ground. The converse is also true but not obvious. Consider the following puzzle: Where does water in a river come from if it has not rained in a while? The water comes from groundwater that has seeped from the aquifer into the river, in what's known as base flow.

Whether water will flow from the river to the aquifer or vice versa depends on the level of the water table in the aquifer and on the elevation of the river. If the water table is above the elevation of the river, water will flow laterally toward the river and augment the flow in the river. In most regions of the country, this is the process that occurs. But as groundwater pumping lowers the water table, the direction of the flow of water changes. Once the water table is below the elevation of the river, water flows from the river toward the aquifer. This is what groundwater pumping did to the Santa Cruz River. It dried up the Santa Cruz by lowering the level of the water table below the elevation of the river. Groundwater pumping literally sucked water from the river and produced horrible environmental consequences. First, of course, the flow in the river disappeared, as did water-dependent species. Then, the trees and shrubs died as groundwater pumping lowered the water table below the root zone of the vegetation.

In Arizona, groundwater pumping has dried up or degraded 90 percent of the state's once perennial desert streams, rivers, and riparian habitats. Some marvelous habitat remains healthy but faces an uncertain future. For example, the San Pedro River is southeastern Arizona supports an estimated 390 species of birds (almost two-thirds of all species seen in North America). The area is so special that Birder's Digest, the Nature Conservancy, the American Bird Conservancy, and the National Audubon Society have given the river special designation. However, the population of the city of Sierra Vista and Cochise County is exploding, and all of this growth is dependant on groundwater. Local politicians and developers fear that environmental issues may retard growth. It is possible that the San Pedro River will suffer the same fate as the Santa Cruz.

Not surprisingly, some developers maintain that groundwater pumping has not caused the lower flow levels in the San Pedro River. To be sure, there will always be a problem of determining the causal relationship between groundwater pumping and environmental degradation. Scientific uncertainty attends many disputes over the impact of pumping on a particular river or spring. Some of this debate is in good faith, an honest disagreement about what the evidence suggests and the computer models predict. Other positions seem animated by gross self-interest. With so much money at stake, developers pay consultants handsome fees to help obtain lucrative permits to pump.

In considering other examples of environmental problems caused by groundwater pumping, the first thing to note is that the impact of groundwater pumping on the environment is not confined to the arid West. Consider Florida. One of the wettest states in the country, with an average of more than 54 inches of rain a year, Florida has always had a problem with water. Historically, the problem was too much water. In a state surrounded on three sides by ocean and with enormous aquifers and extremely high water tables, the problem was how to get rid of the water. Although that story is relatively well known, another version of Florida's water woes is not.

Florida's population jumped from 2.7 million people in 1950 to 16 million in 2000, making Florida the fourth most populous state. A region that is experiencing particularly explosive growth is Tampa Bay. In search of additional supplies during the 1970s, Tampa Bay Water (the local water utility) purchased large tracts of rural areas in adjoining counties and drilled a huge number of wells. By 1996, groundwater withdrawal had risen to approximately 255 million gallons per day, a 400 percent increase over 1960 levels. When lakes and ponds began to dry up—one study found that fewer than 10 of 153 lakes in the region were healthy—Tampa Bay Water knew it had a public relations disaster on its hands. Homeowners who had bought lakefront property only to watch it dry up were not amused. In response, Tampa Bay Water began to dump hundreds of thousands of gallons of water per day into the dry lakebeds. Where did Tampa Bay Water get this additional water? From groundwater pumping. Yet this additional groundwater would inevitably drain back into the ground in search of the water table. It was like trying to keep water in a colander.

Tampa Bay is not the only area where officials have tried to mask the consequences of groundwater pumping. In San Antonio, Texas, Paseo del Rio, or River Walk, has become the city's most popular tourist attraction. A 2.5-mile section of the San Antonio River that flows through the heart of downtown, River Walk anchors a $3.5 billion-per-year tourist industry. Most tourists would be surprised to learn that the river they enjoy is the creation of dams, floodgates, and groundwater pumped from the Edwards Aquifer and dumped into the San Antonio River above River Walk. The San Antonio River was once navigable though the River Walk stretch, but it dried up because of groundwater pumping. In short, the city of San Antonio pumps millions of gallons a day of ground-water into the river in order to create an economically useful fiction. As San Antonio has continued to expand, the San Antonio Water System began to search for new sources of water and to look for ways to reuse existing supplies. In 2000, the system began to dump treated municipal effluent into River Walk as a substitute for groundwater. The water creating the illusion of a real river is still groundwater, but it has been used before.

Americans use groundwater to grow all kinds of things, even when there is no need to do so. Until rather recently, many U.S. farms were "dryland" farmed, meaning that the farmers had no irrigation system. However, Americans' love affair with processed foods caused some potato farmers to shift from dryland to irrigation farming. The problem with dryland potatoes is that their size, shape, and texture depend heavily on seasonal weather patterns. During the growing season, potatoes need constant moisture or they will have knobs and odd shapes. A misshapen or knobby potato is perfectly edible, but it is not an acceptable potato for the fast-food industry. In 1988, McDonald's began to offer consumers "super-sized" meals with larger portions of french fries served in rectangular boxes with flat bottoms. Only potatoes grown through irrigation produced a uniform length fry that would jut out of the super-size box just the right amount so that the consumer could grasp the potato between index finger and thumb and dip it in ketchup. The desire for the perfect fry is felt by the trout in north central Minnesota, where potato farms rely on groundwater that is very closely connected hydrologically to blue-ribbon trout streams. Increased pumping to support additional potato production threatens the survival of trout.

For a final example, consider the country's newfound fascination with bottled water. Sixty percent of Americans drink bottled water, which is now the fastest growing product among the top 50 supermarket categories. Between 1978 and 2001, consumption rose 1,300 percent to 5.4 billion gallons, or about 43 billion 16-ounce bottles. A major beneficiary of the bottled-water craze is the Perrier Group of America. Most consumers know Perrier as the importer of green bottles of spring water from France. But Perrier also sells bottled spring water under 14 other brand names, including Arrowhead, Calistoga, Deer Park, Zephyrhills, Poland Spring, Ozarka, and Ice Mountain. Indeed, Perrier has become the largest U.S. bottler of water (ahead of Pepsi and Coke) with a 32 percent market share. To supply its needs in the United States, Perrier relies on approximately 50 locations around the country, yet it must relentlessly search for new sources to satisfy the growing demand.

One place where Perrier looked was the Mecan River in Wisconsin. A blue-ribbon trout stream, the Mecan has been carefully protected by the state. Beginning in the 1950s, Wisconsin acquired more than 6,000 acres on the Mecan and surrounding tributaries. In 1999, Perrier proposed building a bottling plant and drilling wells on land near Mecan Springs. Environmental groups were aghast at the prospect, for they knew that the cool, underground spring water was critical to the fragile ecology of the river. But under Wisconsin law, the state could not halt Perrier's commercial operation unless the pumping would interfere with the municipal water supply, and it would not. Perrier proposed to pump 720,000 gallons per day from a well located immediately adjacent to the springs. In the end, Perrier decided not to proceed with this plant, in part because of substantial opposition from local residents. However, the problem of the impact of pumping spring water has not gone away. It has simply changed locations. In 2001 and

2002, Perrier opened bottling plants in Tennessee, Michigan, and California.

THE URGENT NEED FOR REFORM

In the United States, the impact of groundwater pumping on the environment is an example of what biologist Garrett Harden called "the tragedy of the commons." The legal rules governing groundwater use encourage exploitation of the resource: They reward rational economic individuals by permitting them to pump enormous quantities of groundwater, regardless of the environmental impact. Most states have failed to eliminate the gap between law and science. In lieu of legal reform, Americans have shown limitless ingenuity in devising technological fixes for water supply problems. These so-called solutions have altered the hydrologic cycle in order to sustain existing usage.

As our water use spirals upward, we must begin to rethink the economic structure by which we value (and usually under-value) our water resources. At the same time, we must act to protect our rivers, springs, wetlands, lakes, and estuaries from groundwater pumping. There is considerable urgency. Because groundwater moves so slowly, it may take years or decades of groundwater pumping before the effect on the environment is apparent. The hidden tragedy and irremediable fact is that groundwater pumping that has already occurred will cause environmental damage in the future.

We must reform the system. A cure will not come quickly or easily, but nature has enormous regenerative capacity. The solution involves charting a new course for the future based on wise policies, then making a commitment to stay the course. It can be done. In the process, state and local governments must play a critical role.

To control the impact of groundwater pumping on the environment, we must combine a command-and-control model of government rules and regulations with the market forces of transferable rights and price incentives. Any meaning-ful reform must do two things: protect the rights of existing users by creating quantified water rights that are transferable and therefore valuable; and break free of the relentless cycle of increasing use by placing restrictions on individual freedom to pump groundwater.

States should foster a market in water rights by allowing the easy transferability of rights from existing users to newcomers. Enormous quantities of groundwater are used for extremely low-value economic activities. State law must facilitate the movement of water from these uses to higher-value ones by establishing a water rights market as the mechanism for accomplishing this shift. But water markets are not the only solution.

Government rules and regulations deserve a prominent place in our reform efforts as we attempt to protect the environment. The states should undertake a number of very specific reforms. First, states should carefully craft water conservation standards. A water conservation program seems, intuitively, like a good idea: Let's save water. However, the experience of some western states with conservation standards sends a mixed message. If the states attempt to impose elaborate and detailed conservation standards, the regulated groups will fight tooth and nail over every sentence in the proposed regulation. This process can consume enormous amounts of time, energy, and money. The lesson for states is that it is better to embrace simple conservation standards that are easy to administer and implement. They are likely to have the most practical effect in terms of actually saving water and will avoid prolonged political struggle. In other words, it is easier to pick low-hanging fruit.

Second, states should establish minimum stream flows and protect those flows from pumping of hydrologically connected groundwater. Through a combination of statutes, judicial decisions, and administrative rules, the state of Washington has developed a system that other states should emulate. The legislature authorized the State Department of Ecology to establish minimum water levels for streams and lakes to protect fish, game, other wildlife resources, and recreational and esthetic values. The minimum levels become appropriations within the prior appropriation system and offer protection against subsequent groundwater pumping.

Third, states should prohibit the drilling of new wells in areas that are hydrologically connected to surface flows. Generally speaking, the farther a well is from a watercourse, the less significant the impact of groundwater pumping from that well will be. States have two options for this problem: They can make the ban on wells near watercourses turn on a hydrologic analysis of the particular region, or they can use a bright-line rule that simply prohibits drilling wells within, for example, a mile of the river. Oregon has moved in this direction.

Fourth, states should impose an extraction tax on water pumped from any well within a certain distance of a river, spring, or lake. This tax would have two benefits: It would encourage existing pumpers to conserve water, and it would create an incentive for new pumpers to locate wells farther away from watercourses.

Fifth, states should require any new pumper to offset or mitigate the impact on the environment. It makes no sense to allow developers to drill new wells in an aquifer already under stress. Arizona has a mitigation program that requires developers to demonstrate an "assured water supply." One way to do so is for the developer to purchase and retire agricultural rights.

Sixth, states, especially through local governments, should use financial incentives as a significant part of water policy. Quite simply, we are not paying the true cost of water. When homeowners or businesses receive a monthly water bill from the utility, that bill normally includes only the extraction costs of drilling the wells, the energy costs of pumping the water, the infrastructure costs of a distribution and storage system, and the administrative costs of the water department or company. Water rates, with rare exceptions, do not include a commodity charge for the water itself. The water is free.

Even though water is a scarce commodity, most Americans have not yet faced the condition that economists call scarcity, which occurs when people alter their consumption patterns in response to price increases. Our habits of water use will not change until the cost of water rises sufficiently to force an alteration. Therefore, we must increase water rates so that all users pay the replacement value of the water, which includes not just the cost of drilling a new well but also the cost of retiring an existing user's well.

Economists agree that significant price increases would create incentives for all users to conserve. All farmers, homeowners, businesses, or industrial users could then decide which uses of water to continue and which to curtail. Rate increases would encourage the elimination of marginal economic activities and the movement of water toward more productive uses.

Seventh, whenever a water rights transfer occurs, the states should require that a small percentage of the water be dedicated for environmental purposes. States should not get too greedy with this environmental dedication, however, or it will be self-defeating. The prospective parties to a transfer will, of course, consider the economic consequence of the dedication on their proposed transfer. If the dedication is too onerous, the sale or lease will not take place. But a modest dedication program has great potential for environmental restoration.

Eighth, both the state and federal governments should commit resources to purchasing and retiring groundwater rights to protect critical watersheds and habitat. Some might argue that the federal government should preempt the area, given how poor a job the states have done. However, Congress has historically deferred to the states with respect to water laws. Proposals for federal regulation of groundwater will give rise to a chorus of howls from states' rights advocates, especially those in the West, who, as author Wallace Stegner once observed, conceive the role of the federal government as "Get out! And give us more money!"

Congress certainly has constitutional authority to impose federal regulations on groundwater pumpers, yet there are two good reasons why it should not do so. First, it would provoke a bruising political battle. The political capital expended to win that fight could be better spent elsewhere. Second, the impact of groundwater pumping on the environment is nuanced and site-specific, depending enormously on the particular hydro-logic characteristics of an aquifer. Imposing a uniform federal template on the nation is likely to exclude some pumping that should be regulated and to include some pumping that poses no serious risk of harm. Offering the carrot of federal funds is a far better approach than wielding the stick of federal regula-tion. Under its taxing and spending power, Congress should create a program funded by federal tax dollars to reward states that protect their environments from groundwater pumping (a gentle form of coercion). A host of federal programs, such as highway funding, give the states money but attach conditions.

The impact of groundwater pumping on the environment is enormous. And it is getting worse. As the drought that is gripping the country continues, cities, farmers, and individual homeowners are scrambling in search of additional water supplies. They have often focused on groundwater; indeed, well-drilling businesses around the country are booming. The drought has prompted the media to pay remarkable attention to water issues. In the summer of 2002, the *New York Times* ran a four-part front-page series, and *U.S. News & World Report*, *Newsweek*, and *National Geographic* ran cover stories. Yet none of these stories, or any others to my knowledge, mentioned that groundwater pumping has environmental consequences.

Does the Clean Water Act Protect the Oceans?

In 1983, the United States staked a claim to the resources of an area larger than the North American continent. President Ronald Reagan created the United States Exclusive Economic Zone, an area that extends 200 miles from U.S. shores and covers nearly 4.5 million square miles.[1] The designation was intended to prevent other countries from taking resources from within the zone.

With this policy came responsibility for protecting the water resource. There are many reasons to protect the oceans. Unregulated use causes economic losses from depleted fisheries, ruined coral reefs, and degraded coastal wetlands. Many people argue that humans should not pollute the oceans because they are a vital part of our ecosystem.

The following article presents the idea that we already have a major policy tool in place to decrease the pollution going into our oceans. Catherine Hazlewood of the Ocean Conservancy's Clean Oceans Program has argued that the Clean Water Act simply needs to be enforced. A major source of pollution is nonpoint source pollution, or the contaminants carried by rain or stormwater. Examples include oils from paved surfaces, fertilizers, animal wastes, and pesticides.[2] Improved monitoring programs for non-point source pollution and comprehensive reduction strategies will improve water quality.

Sound scientific data is an important tool for crafting reasonable resource protection and management policies. In 2001, the U.S. Environmental Protection Agency (EPA) issued the National Coastal Condition Report. The report provided the government's first comprehensive assessment of U.S. coastal conditions. Using existing data, the report found that 44% of American estuaries (places where freshwater mixes with the ocean) is impaired.[3] Yet the Clean Water Act has been in place for over 30 years. Although water quality in the nation has improved, science clearly tells us that the job is not yet done.

—The Editor

1. Pew Oceans Commission. *State of America's Oceans*. 2003.

2. Ibid.

3. U.S. Environmental Protection Agency. *National Coastal Condition Report*. EPA842-F-02-001, December 2001. Available online at *http://www.epa.gov/owow/oceans/nccr/index.html*.

Beneath the Surface
by Cathy Asato

Thirty years after the Clean Water Act mandated healthy water for America, our oceans are still in peril.

On the surface, our oceans look healthy. Waves rhythmically lap onto shore. Beachgoers wade in cool waters. Surfers enthusiastically paddle out in search of the perfect wave, and fishermen dream of landing the big one.

But beneath the surface lies a different story. Despite laws and regulations designed to halt the problem, a host of pollutants render many of our coastal waters unfit for swimming and fishing. Beach closings, fish kills, dead zones, red tides, and bacterial outbreaks are all symptoms of a larger problem—contaminated waters.

Consider the following:

- **44 percent of estuarine areas** are impaired for human use or aquatic plants or animals, says the Environmental Protection Agency (EPA).

- **Unsafe or unhealthy water conditions** prompted 13,410 beach closings or advisories in 2001, according to the Natural Resources Defense Council's (NRDC) annual *Testing the Waters* beach report.

- **Some 80,000 fish died** in a Salt Fork River tributary in central Illinois because of toxic levels of ammonia accidentally flushed into the Urbana sewer system during a boiler cleaning this summer [2002].

- **A runoff-borne parasite** killed 100 people and sickened more than 400,000 in Milwaukee in the summer of 1993.

- **Fishermen near the Florida Keys** reported a large mass of slimy black water almost devoid of marine life earlier this year [2002]. While scientists still cannot pinpoint its origin, many are worried that it is an indicator of the growing impact of human activity along coastlines.

WHAT'S IN OUR WATER AND HOW DID IT GET THERE?

For many years, the unregulated dumping of chemicals, toxins, and other waste directly into lakes, rivers, streams, and oceans triggered disease and other risks to humans and wildlife. In response, Congress passed the Clean Water Act (CWA) in 1972. However, 30 years later, toxins from roads, lawns, farms, sewers, boats, and litter continue to pollute our water.

"Trash is the most visible pollutant on our beaches," explains Catherine Hazlewood, acting director of The Ocean Conservancy's Clean Oceans Program. "However, the real danger lurks in the pollutants that you can't even see."

Hazlewood cites several sources of pollution that, while harmful to the oceans, can go unnoticed by the average person.

POLLUTED RUNOFF

Polluted runoff—contaminated water from streets, parking lots, yards, and farms—falls through the regulatory cracks of CWA, and is the leading source of our water problems today.

Nationwide, agricultural runoff is the most extensive form of water pollution. Rainwater carries pathogenic animal waste, fertilizers, and pesticides over fields and roads into waterways. In addition, ground cesspools, which store animal waste from large feedlots, often flood or leak, sending fecal matter into rivers and streams. Scientists attribute the Gulf of Mexico's infamous dead zone—an area the size of Massachusetts that lacks oxygen, plant, and animal life—to runoff carried by the Mississippi River, which drains some 40 percent of the contiguous 48 states.

But rural areas are not the only polluters. Rainwater washing over city streets, parking lots, and construction sites carries grease, pesticides, litter, and vehicle pollutants to waterways.

SEWAGE TREATMENT PLANTS AND SEPTIC SYSTEMS

Sanitary sewers, designed to carry wastes to treatment plants, malfunction when overloaded, poorly maintained, or obstructed; when this occurs, they dump raw sewage into waterways. Combined sewer systems carry raw sewage and contaminated runoff from city streets to treatment plants. When it rains, they often overflow, diverting untreated waste to the nearest stream or waterway. Last year, sewage spills and overflows accounted for more than 1,880 beach closings or advisories, says NRDC.

OIL SPILLS

Who can forget the images of oil-covered sea birds, fish, and otters following the *Exxon Valdez* spill? What many don't realize is that smaller spills of hazardous wastes frequently occur due to tanker accidents, pipeline breaks, and refinery accidents. In addition, oil from cars, buses, trucks, and other vehicles leaks onto city streets and washes into waterways every time it rains. Over the course of a year, urban runoff from a city of 5 million people can contain as much oil and grease as large tanker spills.

SHIP DISCHARGES

Unlike land-based industries, ships do not need permits for discharges and thus dump sewage, non-sewage wastewater, and ballast water bearing pathogens, invasive species, and other toxics directly into the ocean.

WHAT HAPPENED TO THE CLEAN WATER ACT?

Thirty years ago, Congress enacted one of its most ambitious environmental laws, the Clean Water Act. It proposed "to restore the integrity of the nation's waters." Although it has helped to limit many pollutants, CWA falls short of its "zero discharge goal."

"The Clean Water Act has been a tremendous success in controlling pollution from point sources such as sewage treatment and industrial facilities," says Robert Wayland, director of EPA's Office of Wetlands, Oceans, and Watersheds. "But there are other sources that evade effective control."

EPA has failed to control non-point-source pollution (runoff), and loopholes and exemptions allow ships and agricultural producers to discharge waste without permits or regulations.

"The challenge of writing and enforcing permits for point sources is different from the ones needed to address 2.5 million

What You Can Do

One reason our oceans remain polluted is increasing human use. There are simply more people extracting more resources and consuming more goods. But just as people are responsible for polluting the oceans, we are also the ones who can help. Ordinary citizens can improve ocean water quality by

➤ Conserving water.

➤ Using low phosphate or phosphate-free detergents.

➤ Using natural fertilizers, such as compost, in gardens or on lawns.

➤ Disposing of household toxics, used motor oil, and boating wastes properly.

➤ Keeping litter, waste, and debris out of street gutters and storm drains.

➤ Supporting clean water legislation. Let lawmakers know all Americans deserve clean water. Join The Ocean Conservancy's Ocean Activist Network (*www.oceanconservancy.org*) to receive updates on clean water issues.

farming enterprises and thousands of municipalities," explains Wayland. "It's clear that we need different tools."

But Hazlewood disagrees. She counters that EPA needs to first start using the tools it has. "The biggest problem facing our oceans isn't a lack of available tools, but a lack of political will," she insists.

For example, the Clean Water Act requires enforceable permits to control sewage from large factory farms. However, nationwide, 85 percent of these operations have not received permits from EPA. Wayland admits EPA needs "to raise awareness about how agricultural activity in the upper Midwest can contribute to a dead zone in the Gulf of Mexico."

30 Years of the Clean Water Act

Passed in 1972, the Clean Water Act's (CWA) primary objective, "to protect and restore the physical, chemical, and biological integrity of the nation's waters," established a strong and clear mandate. It proposed to eliminate the discharge of pollutants into the nation's waters and ensure that all rivers, lakes, and coastal waters are safe for activities like swimming and fishing.

CWA gave EPA authority to implement pollution control programs. It required major industries to meet performance standards for waste water, provided financial assistance to states and cities to treat municipal waste, and protected wetlands.

By largely addressing industrial and municipal waste, CWA has made measurable progress. For example, in 1972, 30 to 40 percent of the nation's waters were safe for activities like fishing or swimming. Today, about 60 percent are safe.

Despite its accomplishments, CWA has not fully met its goals. One disappointing statistic: currently, more than 218 million Americans live within 10 miles of a polluted lake, river, stream, or coastal area.

According to Hazlewood, raising awareness is something The Ocean Conservancy tries to help EPA do through its estuarine monitoring workshops, coastal cleanups, and policy advocacy. However, she adds, EPA needs to enforce the laws that protect our oceans and coasts.

Further diluting CWA, Hazlewood says, "The current administration is freezing or rewriting every water quality rule." For example, the Total Maximum Daily Load (TMDL) Program, the only CWA tool that addresses runoff sources, is under attack, she says. It requires states and EPA to identify polluted waterways, rank them for priority attention, and develop pollution limits for each water body. In July 2000, EPA announced regulations to strengthen the program, but in 2001, the Bush administration blocked their implementation and began revising them.

Environmental initiatives also face funding shortages. The Beaches Environmental Assessment and Coastal [Health] Act (BEACH Act), passed in 2000, proposes consistent, nationwide beach water quality standards and requires public notification when standards are exceeded. Currently, only 14 states regularly monitor their beaches at least once a week and notify the public. When Congress passed the act, it authorized $30 million a year for coastal states; this year [2002] the program received only $10 million.

WHAT NEEDS TO BE DONE?

Despite laws and programs aimed at protecting our waters, problems persist, and water quality is worsening. Increased human impact, coupled with decreased public urgency, hampers recovery.

Two major steps to cleaning our oceans include establishing a comprehensive runoff reduction strategy, and increasing and improving water quality monitoring. EPA action to regulate waste and ballast water from shipping is also needed to achieve cleaner waters. Wayland says EPA is talking with Cruise lines on certification programs and regulation.

SIGNS OF HOPE

While lowering our quality of life standards, degraded oceans also pose health and economic risks. Polluted waters containing disease-causing organisms can cause gastroenteritis, dysentery, hepatitis, or respiratory illness. In addition, polluted beaches cost coastal states jobs, productivity, tourism and property tax dollars, and economic growth.

However, several recent initiatives, including the BEACH Act, offer signs of hope that citizens and lawmakers are interested in protecting ocean resources, public health, and local economies. In addition, EPA's first-ever comprehensive *National Coastal Condition Report* has increased attention to coastal water quality by providing the public information on the condition of our aquatic resources.

"Unquestionably, we're better off today than if we had not had a Clean Water Act for the last 30 years," Wayland says. "But there is still a lot of work to be done. We have not exhausted the Act's potential to improve the nation's waters."

Ocean Conservancy Update

The Ocean Conservancy's Clean Oceans Program advocates for stronger laws and increased funding to monitor and enforce existing regulations, and has supported and helped pass legislation such as the BEACH and Oceans Acts. The organization is active in promoting a comprehensive national strategy to reduce runoff pollution, including establishing goals and timetables for runoff reductions in targeted watersheds, restricting application of fertilizers on lawns, golf courses, and public gardens, minimizing runoff from construction sites, and improving wetlands protection.

With regard to CWA, The Ocean Conservancy is in litigation with the federal government over the TMDL [total maximum daily load] program and is working with EPA, states, and associations on setting water quality standards and writing rules for what constitutes public notification.

What Are the Global Policies on Climate Change?

The significance of the Montreal Protocol, signed in 1987, is that it showed that countries can work together to tackle an environmental issue. Countries have reduced the use of ozone-depleting chemicals by 90%. Another effort at international cooperation took place in 1992 when 196 countries met in Rio de Janeiro, Brazil. The purpose of the meeting was to develop strategies to reduce the emissions of greenhouse gases (GHG). The United Nations Framework Convention on Climate Change was "concerned that human activities have been substantially increasing the atmospheric concentrations of greenhouse gases . . . and may adversely affect natural ecosystems and humankind."[1] By May 2004, 189 countries had ratified the agreement.[2]

In 1997, at another international meeting in Kyoto, Japan, many countries signed the Kyoto Protocol. Participating industrialized nations agreed to reduce their GHG emissions. As of July 2004, 84 countries had signed the agreement, and 124 countries had ratified it, or agreed to follow its terms. Interestingly, the United States, the world's largest contributor of GHGs, has not yet ratified the agreement because of economic concerns.

The following excerpt from a 2002 World Watch Institute report, *Reading the Weathervane: Climate Policy from Rio to Johannesburg*, discusses global policies on climate change. (Johannesburg, South Africa, was the site of the 2002 World Summit.) As the report indicates, there is scientific consensus that humans are changing the global climate.[3] Countries are moving toward the goals of the Kyoto Protocol to reduce GHG. The report identifies the variety of methods other countries are taking. Some successful approaches include implementing various economic measures, working with industries, and rallying public support of GHG reduction policies.

Perhaps the largest roadblock to meeting the goals of the Kyoto agreement is the absence of binding legal commitments by countries to reduce GHG. In 2001, Joseph Stiglitz of Columbia University, a Nobel Prize winner for economics, said that significant movement on climate change requires governments to adopt cost-effective domestic climate policies and to set an "agenda for global collective action." Unless the United States ratifies the Kyoto Protocol, the agreement covers only 40% of the global greenhouse gas emissions.[4]

Climate change policies do not just affect the environment. To be successful, policies must address the economic needs and goals of both industrialized and developing nations. As this report concludes, we "can put the world on a more certain path toward climate stability. . . ." The United States has the opportunity to lead the way.

—The Editor

Note: The following article was written before the 2002 World Summit that took place in Johannesburg.

1. United Nations Framework Convention on Climate Change, 2003. Available online at *http://unfccc.int/resource/conv/*.

2. United Nations Framework Convention on Climate Change Website. Available online at *http://www.unfccc.int/resource/convkp.html*.

3. World Watch Institute. *Reading the Weathervane: Climate Policy from Rio to Johannesburg*. World Watch Paper #160, 2002, p. 7.

4. Pew Center on Global Climate Change. *Beyond Kyoto: Advancing the International Effort Against Climate Change*. 2003, p. 1.

Reading the Weathervane: Climate Change from Rio to Johannesburg
by Seth Dunn

INTRODUCTION

Tens of thousands of citizens from government, industry, and civil society around the globe will gather in Johannesburg, South Africa, from August 26 to September 4, 2002, for the World Summit on Sustainable Development. More than 100 heads of state will mark the 10th anniversary of the historic Earth Summit, the 1992 U.N. Conference on Environment and

Development in Rio de Janeiro, Brazil. The summit offers an opportunity not only to assess the world's progress in addressing the broad array of global challenges identified in Rio, but also to mobilize the political will needed for more meaningful action. One question certain to feature prominently at Johannesburg and beyond concerns the future of the Kyoto Protocol to the U.N. Framework Convention on Climate Change (UNFCCC). The original Framework Convention, which was agreed to in Rio and today has 186 member countries, established the objective of stabilizing atmospheric concentrations of greenhouse gases at levels that would avoid "dangerous anthropogenic interference with global climate," thereby minimizing adverse impacts such as rising sea levels, increased storm and flood frequency, the spread of infectious diseases, declines in biodiversity, and reduced availability of food and water. The Framework entered into force in 1994, and three years later, 181 nations meeting in Kyoto, Japan, agreed to the Kyoto Protocol, which would commit ratifying industrial nations to collectively reduce their emissions of these gases by 5 percent between 1990 and 2008–12.

For the next three years, progress in finalizing the rules for implementing the Kyoto pact flagged. But new life was inadvertently breathed into the negotiations by the U.S. administration's withdrawal from the talks in early 2001, which galvanized Europe, Japan, Canada, and other industrial nations to resolve their points of contention. With the United States absent from the negotiating table, the remaining 180 nations worked out most of the outstanding issues at meetings in Bonn, Germany, and Marrakech, Morocco, in mid- and late-2001. (See Box on pages 99–100.)

As the Johannesburg Summit nears, whether or when the Kyoto Protocol will enter into force is fueling an international debate. This evokes a twinge of *déjà vu* when compared with the debate that preceded Rio, when the issue at hand was whether the original Framework treaty would be signed. Now, as then, the European Union (EU) leads the push to bring Kyoto into force, arguing that mandatory reductions in greenhouse gas emissions are essential. Now, as then, a U.S. administration led by a President George Bush resists European entreaties, citing concern that the terms under discussion might be unduly harmful to the U.S. economy. And now, as then, environmental NGOs [nongovernmental organizations] furnish rosy studies projecting an economic boom if the agreement were to be ratified, while industry associations promote dire predictions of bust.

Beneath the surface of these superficial similarities, however, the environment of climate policymaking has undergone a sea change since 1992. At the time of the Rio summit, considerable scientific uncertainty existed as to whether human activities, rather than natural factors, could be conclusively implicated in ongoing changes in the Earth's climate. The costs of reducing greenhouse gas emissions were widely anticipated by economists to be very high, and the potential of new technologies to achieve substantial emissions cuts was only beginning to be calculated. For these reasons among others, most businesses were skeptical

The U.N. Framework Convention on Climate Change and the Kyoto Protocol

The U.N. Framework Convention on Climate Change (UNFCCC), which was signed at the 1992 Rio Summit and entered into force in March 1994, established the objective of stabilizing atmospheric concentrations of greenhouse gases at levels that will avoid "dangerous anthropogenic interference with global climate" and allow economic development to proceed. The UNFCCC recognizes several basic principles: that scientific uncertainty must not be used to avoid precautionary action; that nations have "common but differentiated responsibilities"; and that industrial nations, with the greatest historical contribution to climate change, must take the lead in addressing the problem. The agreement commits all signatory nations to address climate change, adapt to its effects, and report on the actions they are taking to implement the Convention. It requires industrial countries and economies in transition—Annex I nations— to formulate and submit regular reports detailing their climate policies and their greenhouse gas inventories. And it requires Annex I nations to aim for a voluntary goal of returning emissions to 1990 levels by the year 2000, and to provide technical and financial assistance to developing, or non-Annex I, nations. Today, 181 nations and the European Union (EU) are party to the UNFCCC.

In 1995, signatories to the UNFCCC concluded that its existing commitments were inadequate for meeting its objective and launched talks toward a legally binding agreement that would establish emissions reduction commitments for industrial nations. These negotiations culminated in the 1997 Kyoto Protocol, which collectively commits industrial and former Eastern bloc nations—termed "Annex B" nations—to reduce their greenhouse gas emissions by 5.2 percent below 1990 levels during the period 2008–2012, and to demonstrate "meaningful progress" toward this goal by 2005. The agreement includes several measures designed to lessen the difficulty of meeting the target, such as the inclusion of six greenhouse gases and "flexibility mechanisms" that allow emissions trading, the use of forests and other carbon "sinks," and the earning of credits through overseas Clean Development Mechanism and joint implementation projects. It also commits all UNFCCC signatories to further advance their commitments to address greenhouse gas emissions.

In 1998, negotiators agreed to a plan of action and timeline for finalizing the rules surrounding the Protocol's specifics. At talks in the Hague in late 2000, disagreement between the United States and the EU over several key provisions led to a breakdown in the talks. Following the U.S. withdrawal from the negotiating process in March 2001, a total of 180 nations finalized most of the "rulebook" for implementing the Protocol during talks in Bonn, Germany, and Marrakech, Morocco. Many of these details—placing no limit on trading, for example, or allowing credits from afforestation and reforestation—will allow countries more flexibility in meeting their Kyoto targets. The next round of negotiations will be held in New Delhi, India, from 23 October to 1 November 2002.

of the science of climate change and questioned the need for an international response. And the political clout of the United States, dampened by a recession and an unsympathetic administration, was sufficient to water down the initial framework agreement.

Ten years later [in 2002], the landscape is fundamentally different. A broad scientific consensus now confirms that human induced climate change is not only under way, but accelerating. Debate over the economics of climate change has broadened, in recognition of the ability of new technologies and policies to change conventional assumptions about the cost of reducing emissions. Wind and solar power, fuel cells and hydrogen, and other emerging energy technologies and fuels have entered or are nearing the marketplace, spawning nascent multibillion-dollar industries while dramatically improving prospects for a "decarbonized," low-greenhouse-gas energy economy. A growing number of corporations have moved beyond denial to acceptance of the science of climate change and have begun to act—seeking competitive advantage by anticipating future policy changes rather than resisting or reacting to them, in the belief that this approach will both reduce the long-run costs and increase the long-run benefits associated with action.

But the most significant development of all is that the international community may now have the multilateral momentum to bring the 1997 Kyoto Protocol into force—leaving the unilateralist United States standing on the sidelines.

The European Union and its 15 member states, and Japan, gave the process a major boost with their ratifications in May and early June 2002. Should Russia and Canada follow suit—as they are expected to do—the conditions for the Protocol's entry into force would be satisfied. (See Box on page 102.)

Amid these promising shifts in the political winds of change, it is helpful—and sobering—to remember that the Rio agreement, for all its initial promise, did little to keep global climate-related trends from heading in the wrong direction during the 1990s. Global carbon emissions set several new

Annex I Parties

SHARE OF ANNEX I PARTY

Party	1990 Share of Carbon Emissions (%)
U.S.	36.1
EU-15	24.2
Russia	17.4
Japan	8.5
Poland	3.0
Other Europe	5.2
Canada	3.3
Australia	2.1
New Zealand	0.2
Total	100.0

ANNEX I PARTIES THAT HAVE RATIFIED THE KYOTO PROTOCOL, JUNE 2002

Party	1990 Share of Carbon Emissions (%)
EU-15	24.2
Japan	8.5
Czech Republic	1.2
Romania	1.2
Slovakia	0.4
Norway	0.3
Iceland	0.0
Total	35.8

highs, while nearly all countries fell short of their initial Rio goals. New records in global carbon dioxide (CO_2) concentrations and global temperature were also established, suggesting that the gap between climate science and policy has widened, rather than narrowed, since Rio.

At the same time, it would be a mistake to conclude—simply on the basis of these broader global trends—that climate policy has stood still, and that there is nothing to be learned from these last 10 years. In fact, hundreds of climate-related policies have been developed and adopted in many countries around the world. Understanding what has worked, what has not, and what has yet to be tried may be useful to countries now preparing to implement the Kyoto Protocol.

Despite its potential value, remarkably little effort has been devoted to evaluating the recent history of climate policy or to extracting its lessons, as this paper attempts to do. It begins by outlining how the environment of climate policymaking has changed over the past decade. It then analyzes and assesses the development and implementation of climate policy between Rio and Johannesburg in different countries, focusing on policies to reduce carbon emissions from the energy sector—the most important greenhouse gas and sector, respectively. It homes in on the experiences of 11 industrial and developing nations and one region—countries selected for their dominant influence on global carbon emissions trends (collectively, they put out more than two thirds of the global total), their prominent roles in international climate diplomacy, and their economic and geographic diversity.

The experience of this group is not only of historical interest—it carries momentous implications for climate policy.

HOW CAN THE KYOTO PROTOCOL ENTER INTO FORCE?

The Kyoto Protocol does not become an instrument of international law until it is brought into force. For this to occur, 55 parties, representing 55 percent of Annex I parties' carbon emissions in 1990, must ratify the agreement. As of early June 2002, the Protocol had been ratified by 74 parties. The majority of these are developing nations, including Argentina, Mexico, Senegal, and small island states such as Trinidad and Tobago.

But the total also includes 21 Annex I parties, including the 15 member states of the EU, Japan, and several other European parties. With the U.S. unlikely to ratify in the near future, entry into force will require ratification by Russia and another party, possibly Canada or Poland.

Ten years ago, in Rio, it was widely believed that a voluntary aim—to return industrial-nation emissions to 1990 levels by 2000—would be a sufficient first step toward achieving the treaty's broader objective of climate stabilization. But with the benefit of a decade of hindsight, as the country studies that follow illustrate, it is evident that the entirely voluntary approach of the 1992 Rio framework treaty failed to motivate either effective domestic climate policy, or the international coordination of climate-related actions.

More specific lessons can be extracted from the early evolution of climate policy as well. The paper identifies several "good practices" that have been successful in areas such as fossil fuel subsidy reform and carbon taxes, energy efficiency, and support for renewable energy. It also points out "perverse practices" that have worked against the goal, most notably the tenacity of direct and indirect fossil fuel subsidies and the virtual neglect by most governments of the transport sector—the fastest-growing source of emissions.

Based on these case studies, it is clear that governments are experimenting with many climate policies, and that some are having a modest impact on emissions. But the aggregate impact of these efforts has been relatively slight, for several reasons: Many policies have been incompletely adopted, weak, or not fully implemented; many have not been coordinated with other measures or integrated with policies in other sectors; and few have been widely replicated. This indicates the need for governments to take a broader, more aggressive approach to climate policy.

This assessment also finds compelling evidence to dispel the notion promoted by Western opponents of climate change agreements that developing countries like China and India, which do not have binding commitments to limit emissions under the first round of Kyoto targets, are "rogue nation" emitters, undermining global climate goals. To the contrary, the study found developing nations, in advance of binding requirements to reduce emissions, already taking numerous actions to restrain emissions growth—largely for economic reasons.

Their experience dramatizes the need for governments to better account for the "ancillary" economic benefits of cutting greenhouse gas emissions—such as reduced air pollution, energy cost savings, lower government expenditures, and the creation of new industries and jobs. The failure to factor in such benefits is but one of many flawed assumptions in the models of some economists, which project forbiddingly high costs from climate policy even as on-the-ground realities increasingly show such predictions to be highly exaggerated.

This decade of experience shows that the lack of industrial-country leadership in demonstrating the need to reduce emissions has been the largest obstacle to effective national and international climate policymaking. Recognition of this problem leads directly to the conclusion that the ratification and entry into force of the Kyoto Protocol would be the single most critical action needed to close the widening gap between climate science and climate policy—both internationally and nationally. Such a step would signal the renewed commitment by industrial-nation governments to the leadership role they signed up for in Rio, and prompt the private sector to prepare for accelerated development and market commercialization of clean energy technologies.

Bringing Kyoto into force would also be the best means of reengaging the U.S. government and private sector on this issue, and of setting the stage for discussing and phasing in fair, binding developing-nation commitments at a later stage. It would establish the global framework that is essential for ensuring that innovative and effective climate policy options—carbon taxation, emissions trading, overseas "clean development" projects—are internationally coordinated and widely implemented. And it would demonstrate, as one diplomat describing the recent revival of climate negotiations put it, "the triumph of multilateralism over unilateralism" in dealing with one of our most pressing global challenges. . . .

CONCLUSION AND RECOMMENDATIONS

Only a few leading emitters—the United Kingdom, Germany, Russia—have met their Rio goals and are on course to meet their Kyoto goals. But as the case studies illustrate, most national governments of industrial countries are stepping up their activity in the area of climate policy. Indeed, the IEA [International Energy Agency] has identified more than 300 separate measures that its members undertook during 1999 to address climate change. The agency placed these actions in five general categories: fiscal policy, market policy, regulatory policy, R&D [research and development] policy, and policy processes, and noted that "good practice" climate policies should:

- maximize both economic efficiency and environmental protection;

- be politically feasible;

- minimize red tape and overhead; and

- have positive effects on other areas, such as competition, trade, and social welfare.

Using these principles to examine the current record, one can identify several good practices to date. (See Table on page 107.)

While there is no "silver bullet" climate policy that can be applied across all countries, experience to date suggests that getting the prices right through subsidy reform and tax policy is crucial. Market approaches and a mix of policies—voluntary agreements, standards, incentives, R&D—are also needed. Important as well are monitoring and assessment, good institutions, and international cooperation. Even if their rationale is strong, however, climate policies run into the formidable barriers of perceived high cost and limited political will to act— as has been demonstrated in many of the studies above.

Climate-related fiscal policies have become increasingly popular, with nearly all industrial countries adopting such measures, though most are modest in size. These measures are appealing because they tend to reduce greenhouse gas emissions while stimulating national economies. A good example is the phasedown of coal subsidies in Belgium, Japan, Portugal, and the United Kingdom from more than $13 billion in 1990 to less than $7 billion by the end of the decade. Subsidies are also being added to promote more-efficient vehicles and renewable energy in power generation, the most successful example to date being the German electricity feed law—which has spurred the wind power business and been replicated in several other European nations.

Nineteen industrial nations are planning more than 60 tax policy changes that will affect emissions, although only 11 of

Policies and Practices

CATEGORY POLICIES	"GOOD PRACTICES" TO DATE
Fiscal ecotaxes	Norway, Sweden carbon taxes
Tax credits or exemptions	U.S. wind power tax credit
Subsidy reform	U.K. coal subsidy removal
Market emissions trading	U.K., Denmark emissions trading programs
Regulatory mandates/standards	Germany electricity feed law
Voluntary agreements	Germany, Netherlands agreements
Labeling	U.S. Energy Star program
R&D funding and incentives	Japan renewable energy funding
Technology development	Japan energy efficiency program
Policy processes strategic planning	U.K. climate change program

these are defined as carbon or emissions taxes. The most effective carbon taxes to date are in Scandinavia: One example discussed in the previous section, Norway's levy, was adopted in 1991 and has reportedly lowered carbon emissions from power plants by 21 percent. One reason such taxes have been adopted slowly or contain exemptions is that their impact on fairness and competitiveness is often overstated by industry.

Interest in market-based mechanisms has also risen, due to their expected cost-effectiveness and the success of the U.S. sulfur emissions trading program, which has helped to reduce sulfur emissions by 24 percent since the program was instituted in 1990. Several countries, along with the European Union, have adopted greenhouse gas emissions trading proposals, and a growing number are considering their adoption. As a recent Pew Center study on Global Climate Change reports, emissions trading is becoming a "policy of choice" for addressing the issue. An international greenhouse gas market is emerging—an estimated 85–105 million tons of CO_2 equivalent have been traded since 1996, nearly half of this in 2001 alone—but in the absence of an international agreement, it is evolving in fragmented fashion. As noted earlier, the U.K., Danish, and EU systems vary considerably in approach, and it will be necessary to reconcile them into a global framework if the trading is to be as economically and environmentally effective as possible.

The third discernible area of growing activity is voluntary agreements, which arise from negotiations between government and business or industry associations. These are attractive because they arouse less political resistance from industry than coercive measures, require little overhead, and can be complemented by fiscal and regulatory measures. Some 21 voluntary agreements were initiated in 1999 by industrial nations, including four for power generation, two for transport, and 11 for industry and manufacturing. With respect to stringency, they are characterized by the IEA as "strong" (in the Netherlands), containing legally binding objectives and the threat of regulation for noncompliance; "weak" (in Canada), lacking penalties for noncompliance but having incentives for achieving the targets; or "cooperative" (in U.S. manufacturing), with incentives for developing and implementing new technology but lacking specific targets.

While voluntary agreements are relatively new, some interesting results have already emerged. As shown above, the German and Japanese business communities have made substantial progress in meeting efficiency targets. Also worth mentioning are the Netherlands' long-term agreements with energy-intensive industry, which achieved a 20 percent energy efficiency improvement between 1989 and 2000. UNEP [United Nations Environment Program] and the World Energy Council (WEC) have identified more than 700 voluntary projects to cut back greenhouse gas emissions that are just completed, under way, or planned by industry. These have achieved a reduction of 1.3 billion tons of CO_2 equivalent, and a 2 billion ton target has been set for 2010. But UNEP and WEC believe that even as industry activity grows, governments remain too reactive—suggesting that industry could, given the right framework, move much faster than is encouraged by current government arrangements.

While these studies suggest growing engagement by industrial-nation governments in dealing with climate change, the IEA observes that "there remains considerable scope for further improvements." The IEA concludes that policies already enacted and proposed may not suffice for countries to meet their Kyoto targets, and that further action may be necessary. These conclusions are consistent with those drawn from the country studies described above.

In addition to identifying good practices, it is also critical, in evaluating climate policy over the past decade, to compare governments' broader approaches with those recommended by the IPCC [Intergovernmental Panel on Climate Change] literature and described in the second section of the paper. In other words, we need to ask: Did countries take a "portfolio" approach to climate policy, emphasizing a mix of instruments? Did they integrate policies with the non-climate objectives of other social and economic policies? Did they account for the ancillary benefits of policies that cut emissions? Did they coordinate actions inter-nationally? And did they follow the principle that earlier action provides greater flexibility in moving toward long-term goals?

Applying these yardsticks to the country studies, we find that:

- Efforts to develop a balanced, "diversified portfolio" of policies are incomplete, with many governments relying mainly on one type of measure.

- Integration of climate change with the non-climate objectives of other policies has been highly limited.

- There has been little effort to assess the ancillary benefits of policies that reduce emissions.

- Few actions have been coordinated internationally.

- An emphasis on the importance of early action is not evident.

Why have countries largely failed to follow these IPCC recommendations? There are, of course, many reasons that partly explain this divergence between the theory and practice of climate policy. As the previous sections show, climate policy-making is still immature, and the varying quality and quantity of information provided by governments—on the policies developed, their level of implementation, and their actual and projected impacts on emissions—make it difficult to assess what is being attempted, much less what is really being done, and what the impact has been. Therefore, continued progress in the reporting and review of national climate policy is needed. In particular, a more rigorous accounting of the specific emissions impacts of individual policies is required to assess which policies are most effective—and to enable the broader replication of the good practices that do exist.

To the extent that one can accurately compare the climate policies of different countries, it is evident that some are measuring up better than others. The degree of commitment to the climate change issue ranges widely among governments, for several reasons. In some countries, public awareness of the seriousness of the issue is strong, while in others there is still only a vague understanding. In some countries, the issue has broad political support; in others, it divides sharply along party lines. These cultural factors help explain why, for example, the United Kingdom, German, and Japanese policies are clearly more integrated than those of Australia, Canada, and the United States. Equally evident, however, is that all countries could be doing much better with respect to each of the climate policy benchmarks.

We have also learned that effective climate policymaking can be weakened by the misuse of projections. In the case of the United States, overly optimistic projections of business-as-usual emissions trends—based on unrealistic assumptions about economic growth and energy prices—led to the development of inadequate policies. Of these policies, a number were partially implemented or discontinued, resulting in even lower emissions cuts than expected. This combination of events caused U.S. emissions to balloon over the past decade. In the future, governments must resist the temptation to misrepresent the future in order to justify present climate policy.

We have seen as well that climate-related policies can be simply overwhelmed by often longstanding "perverse practices" in the energy and transport sectors. Fossil fuel subsidies in many countries keep the cost of these fuels artificially low and continue to greatly inhibit more climate-friendly patterns of energy use. It is hardly surprising that the countries struggling most with emissions—the United States, Canada, and Australia—exemplify the frontier mentality vis-à-vis climate policy, continuing to distort prices for fossil fuels as if they and the atmosphere's absorptive capacity for carbon were limitless. By contrast, even limited efforts toward subsidy removal and carbon taxation in Europe have yielded results in reducing emissions.

Also falling into the category of perverse practices are the numerous subsidies for road building, suburban development, and car travel that permeate the developed world—particularly North America, but to an increasing extent Europe as well. The

OECD [Organization for Economic Cooperation and Development] estimates that removing direct and indirect transport subsidies would reduce sectoral emissions by 10–15 percent.

Indeed, the transport sector has been a major blind spot in climate policy since Rio, receiving very little attention while becoming the fastest-growing source of emissions. This is a political problem, owing to the breadth of issues bearing on transport and industrial resistance to a strengthening of automobile fuel economy standards. But it will become increasingly important, as transport is projected to remain the fastest-growing source of emissions through 2020.

These perverse practices also create a perceptual problem: Those countries formulating new climate policies have by and large failed to acknowledge those policies that undermine efforts to address climate change, much less advocate their reform. Indeed, in just one country report examined in preparing this paper—that of Sweden—did we find a section discussing "policies that run counter to the objective of reducing greenhouse gas emissions." For climate policymakers to overcome these obstacles, they must do a better job of recognizing their existence more explicitly, and employ economic arguments to overcome political inertia.

Tackling transport, something that industrial nations have yet to do, will be an urgent necessity for developing-nation governments as their climate policies evolve. Transport emissions are projected to grow fastest in the developing world, as these nations continue to experience rapid population growth, urbanization, and increased motorization. Yet there are a range of policies and strategies—road pricing, public transit investment, land use planning—to slow these rates of growth, many of which will also alleviate local air pollution, congestion, and road infrastructure expenditures. This will require learning from the experiences—and mistakes—of the industrialized world in their transportation investments.

Another obstacle to better climate policy has been the reluctance in some quarters to acknowledge the climate-related efforts of developing nations. One of the enduring myths of

Kyoto, perpetuated largely by opponents of the Protocol in the United States, is that developing nations would be exempt from any commitments because they lacked the same binding targets.

What the case studies suggest, on the contrary, is that, even before such targets are set for them, developing nations are moving to address their emissions—more, some have argued, than many industrial nations. In a 1999 report for the U.N. Development Programme, José Goldemberg and Walter Reid assert that "clearly, developing countries are not passive spectators in the arena of climate change. They have already taken significant steps to reduce their emissions of greenhouse gases below the levels that would otherwise occur." These countries' experiences demonstrate that many steps to reduce emissions make sense on economic grounds alone—a lesson that could be usefully exported from South to North.

But among the many impediments to effective climate policymaking in industrial and developing nations alike, the one looming largest has been the absence of leadership among industrial nations to agreed to binding, specific commitments to reduce emissions. Indeed, the evidence here makes it abundantly clear that the purely voluntary approach of the Rio treaty failed to promote strong domestic climate policymaking over the past decade, and was therefore not up to the job of promoting meaningful progress toward reducing global carbon emissions. This conclusion, in turn, points to the vital importance of a global—and binding—framework to coordinate and accelerate action on climate change.

Increasingly, the need to globally coordinate climate policy has been accepted and advocated by distinguished economists. Joseph Stiglitz of Columbia University argues in a 2001 paper—released the day after he won the Nobel Prize in economics—that significant movement on climate change requires that governments move on two fronts: to adopt cost-effective domestic climate policies and to set an "agenda for global collective action." William Nordhaus of Yale University, who has criticized the Kyoto Protocol as being potentially expensive, nonetheless concedes in a November

2001 issue of *Science* that the treaty's mechanisms will "provide valuable insights on how complicated international environmental programs will work. . . . It is hard to see why the United States should not join with other countries in paying for this knowledge."

Reengaging the world's largest emitter in the Kyoto process will be difficult, but essential. Richard Schmalensee, Dean of MIT's Sloan School of Management, writes that "the longer the United States, other industrialized nations, and the developing world head down different policy tracks on global warming, the harder it will be to achieve the coordination necessary for effective action." But the purely voluntary approach of the Bush administration seems unlikely to change in the near future, notwithstanding the fact that such an approach, which was already questionable under the first President Bush during the 1992 Rio talks, is far less defensible today, with a decade of policy history under our belts. Indeed, we can now confidently discard the claim made in 1992—and recycled today—that soft, voluntary aims would get us where we need to go. To continue to make this case betrays either policy amnesia or willful neglect of the record of the past 10 years.

U.S. climate policy also places political expediency over economics in ignoring the recent success of its sulfur emissions trading experience. This program set a goal of reducing sulfur dioxide (SO_2) emissions by 10 million tons below the 1980 level, tightening restrictions in two phases. In the first year of compliance, 1995, the program cut sulfur emissions 40 percent below the level required by law. Since then, SO_2 emissions have been dropping steadily, as has the cost of the reductions. To date, the program's cost has been one fifth to one tenth of the $15 billion estimate made in 1990 by the Congress and Environmental Protection Agency.

In its 2002 Economic Report of the President, the administration's own Council of Economic Advisors (CEA) notes that the sulfur emissions trading program "has lowered emissions substantially while yielding considerable cost savings, especially compared with the previous, command-and-control regime." It adds that "as low-cost options for emission reduction emerged that had not been foreseen in 1989, there has been over time a clear downward trend in the predicted cost of the program." Yet the report is surprisingly skeptical about applying these lessons to climate policy, calling an international greenhouse gas trading system "impractical" and arguing that "a flexible international program would be unprecedented."

Ironically, CEA Chair R. Glenn Hubbard had proposed, unsuccessfully, the inclusion of mandatory emissions caps and tradeable permits in the administration's climate policy. At the moment, however, Hubbard is limited to abstractly advocating the use of "flexible institutions" to deal with climate change, even as such institutions are being built overseas.

Conventional arguments against the Protocol—that it would be too costly, and that it excludes developing nations—are also belied by our experience in addressing another global environmental problem. It was under the Reagan administration that the U.S. government signed and ratified the 1985 Vienna Convention and 1987 Montreal Protocol to address ozone-layer depletion. As Edward Parson of Harvard's Kennedy School of Government points out, the first round of the Montreal Protocol did not include binding commitments from China, India, and other developing nations. These commitments were phased in during subsequent amendments, and since 1987 the Protocol has achieved a 90 percent reduction in the use of ozone-depleting chlorofluorocarbons, and at a modest cost.

Finally, the common assumption that U.S. businesses will benefit from their government's unwillingness to ratify the Protocol deserves closer examination. In the near term, there may be some advantages over foreign competitors subject to constraints. But over the long term, the ongoing policy uncertainty may have an adverse impact, particularly if other countries' climate policies spur technological innovation, open up new markets, and create a global trading system in which U.S. firms are unable to participate.

There are ways in which separate U.S. and international strategies might eventually converge. Various proposals for a

U.S. national cap-and-trade program for carbon are being considered within the administration and Congress. One of these proposals, from Richard Morgenstern of Resources for the Future, would combine elements of a tax and trading system to allay concerns that carbon prices may skyrocket. Meanwhile, legal amendments to the Protocol could allow the permits that result from such a program to be recognized in the Kyoto system, and for Kyoto permits to be recognized in the U.S. system.

But this could create significant complications for multi-nationals operating within and outside the United States—and could require agreement to certain terms dictated by governments that are already party to the Protocol, just as countries seeking to join the World Trade Organization must demonstrate adherence to certain internationally accepted norms.

These challenges, and the failure of the United States to provide a credible alternative to Kyoto, lend weight to the argument of U.K. climate policy expert Michael Grubb that the Kyoto Protocol remains the best way to achieve global action on climate change. Grubb argues that if the EU leads an international effort, joining with Japan and Russia, to bring the Protocol into force, then the United States will be under greater pressure to rejoin. This would also, he concludes, provide a long-term structure for controlling emissions and strengthen the international framework for continuing action. Further, it would also demonstrate industrial-country leadership, making it easier to bring other nations on board at a later date; and it would bring to the private sector the certainty it seeks—and needs—regarding regulations and targets in order to foster the technological development and spread of energy-efficient and low-carbon technologies.

Indeed, achieving the entry into force of the Kyoto Protocol at the earliest possible date will maximize the options for governments and businesses to map out strategies for meeting the Kyoto goals and for making progress toward the broader goal of climate stabilization. Bringing the Kyoto Protocol into force is one of several pressing priorities for advancing the global climate change agenda at and beyond the Johannesburg

Summit. (See Box below.) It is also, at this critical juncture, the single most important action needed to strengthen climate policy at both the national and international levels.

International climate policy would also benefit from a specific long-term goal, on which scientists have yet to agree. In a June 2002 issue of *Science*, Brian O'Neill of Brown University and Michael Oppenheimer of Princeton University propose a stabilization target of 450 ppmv [parts per million by volume]—but note that this option would be foreclosed by further delay in reducing industrial nation emissions. They thus conclude that the Kyoto accord "provides a first step that may be necessary for avoiding dangerous climate interference."

Global Climate Policy Priorities, Johannesburg and Beyond

➤ Bring the Kyoto Protocol into force.

➤ Fully account for climate change in reviewing Agenda 21 implementation in the areas of atmosphere, energy, finance, industry, and technology.

➤ Reaffirm the importance of the IPCC Third Assessment Report as the authoritative starting point for policymakers seeking to implement the Kyoto Protocol.

➤ Set forth a blueprint for post-Johannesburg climate negotiations, emphasizing the need to reengage the United States, begin discussing the second period of emissions cuts, and expand the group of countries with emissions targets.

➤ Work to establish a voluntary "Global Climate Compact," modeled after the Global Compact established in 2000 between the U.N. and the private sector, that challenges business leaders to commit to the accelerated deployment of energy-efficient products, renewable energy, and hydrogen and fuel cell technologies.

Though climate policymaking is still young, a decade of hindsight has made at least two things clear: Climate change has established itself on the radarscreen of policymakers around the globe, and it will not be going away any time soon. As Thomas Schelling observes in the May/June 2002 issue of *Foreign Affairs,*

> The greenhouse gas issue will persist through the entire century and beyond. Even though the developed nations have not succeeded in finding a collaborative way to approach the issue, it is still early. We have been at it for only a decade. But time should not be wasted getting started. Global climate change may become what nuclear arms control was for the past half century. It took more than a decade to develop a concept of arms control. It is not surprising that it is taking that long to find a way to come to consensus on an approach to the greenhouse problem.

Consensus—at least for this stage of the debate, and for most of the world's governments—may be closer than Schelling thinks. We are living in a moment when the need for multilateral action to address emerging global threats is widely accepted by the international community. Unfortunately, it required the tragic terrorist attacks of September 11, 2001, to shock the public and policymakers out of complacency, and to spur the necessary and long overdue changes in counterterrorism policy at home and abroad. We need not wait for a disastrous climate surprise—a deadly heat wave, a particularly destructive storm, a nearly unmanageable tropical disease outbreak—to move us beyond our current state of complacency and toward the many needed reforms. By implementing the Kyoto Protocol, and by working to further raise public awareness of our vulnerability, we can put the world on a more certain path toward climate stability, and set in motion a second decade of climate policy that builds on the lessons of the first yet is far more successful.

How Are Our States and Cities Addressing Climate Change?

Global climate change is just that—global: The effects are felt all over the planet. Carbon dioxide, a major greenhouse gas, mixes throughout the atmosphere. Changes in weather patterns, rising sea levels, droughts, and floods are all observable effects of global warming. Most scientists agree that humans are causing climate change to accelerate.[1] An international convention in Rio de Janeiro in 1992 and another in Kyoto, Japan, in 1997 demonstrated the commitment of industrial nations to reduce the emissions of greenhouse gases. To date, the United States has not ratified the Kyoto Agreement. Germany, Russia, and the United Kingdom have met the goals set in 1992 and are working toward meeting their Kyoto emission reduction goals.[2]

As the following article discusses, many U.S. states are not waiting for the federal government, which favors a voluntary approach, to help reduce greenhouse gas (GHG) emissions. Although states may not pass laws that violate or are less strict than federal regulations, they may choose to put in place stronger regulations to protect the environment. States may also sue companies or the federal government in effort to reduce pollution or to strengthen regulations. Could state action make a difference? Perhaps. Consider that the states of Texas and California combined emit more GHG than the entire continent of Africa.

In July 2004, officials from eight states and New York City filed a lawsuit in an effort to force five utility companies to reduce their carbon dioxide emissions.[3] In June 2004, California announced its intention to cut vehicle GHG emissions by 30%. The governor of West Virginia, a state with an energy-based economy, included this thought in his 2004 State of the State message: "We can no longer bury our head in the sand on the issue of greenhouse gases . . . we must continue to take a leadership role on climate change issues."[4]

Authors Susan Joy Hassol and Randy Udall explain that it is not only the states that are involved. Cities and corporations are working toward reducing GHG emissions, too. There is still a great deal for the federal government to do. But the actions of individuals, cities, companies, and states demonstrate a deepening national commitment to slow global warming.

—The Editor

1. Pew Center on Global Climate Change. *Beyond Kyoto: Advancing the International Effort Against Climate Change.* 2003, p. 1.

2. World Watch Institute. *Reading the Weathervane: Climate Policy from Rio to Johannesburg.* World Watch Paper #160, 2002, p. 71.

3. Pew Center for Global Climate Change. *State News.* July 2004. Available online at *http://www.pewclimate.org/what_s_being_done/in_the_states/news.cfm.*

4. Ibid.

A Change of Climate
by Susan Joy Hassol and Randy Udall

Despite a lack of leadership from the federal government, a ground swell of activity to cut emissions of greenhouse gases is emerging throughout the United States.

Although the signs of global warming are becoming ever more prominent, casual observers of the media in the United States or Europe might easily conclude that U.S. citizens are in denial about climate change, refusing to take responsibility for controlling their emissions of carbon dioxide (CO_2) and the other greenhouse gases (GHGs) that cause global warming. Although it is true that the federal government remains stalemated on how to deal with climate change, the notion that no climate action is taking place in this country is erroneous. The most intriguing story is what has been happening in state legislatures, at city council meetings, and in corporate boardrooms, as well as on college campuses, in community groups, and in a range of other local settings. Across the nation, numerous climate action programs are moving aggressively to reduce emissions of GHGs.

It is rare that a week goes by without the announcement of a new initiative. Among recent clippings, New York Governor George Pataki, a Republican, announced that his state aims to get 25 percent of its electricity from carbon-free renewable energy resources within a decade. Ford and General Motors declared their intent to follow Toyota's lead and manufacture hybrid electric cars and trucks that are more fuel-efficient and less polluting. New Hampshire adopted emissions controls for three aging power plants. American Electric Power, the largest single source of GHGs in the western world, launched an effort to reduce its emissions by 4 percent by 2006. Students at Zach Elementary School in Ft. Collins, Colorado, choose to purchase wind energy instead of coal power, thus keeping 420,000 pounds of CO_2, the leading GHG, out of the atmosphere. How many millions of tons of CO_2 have been saved by the activities of states, cities, corporations, and citizens has not yet been calculated, but the number is growing rapidly.

What is the significance of this nascent grassroots movement? In the past, major shifts in societal values have originated at the local level. Popular movements to abolish slavery, allow women to vote, extend civil rights to African Americans, and curb secondhand smoke started small and then spread nationally. The nation now seems to be witnessing a similar snowball effect, where one successful climate action program inspires two or three more. These early efforts are demonstrating that climate protection is possible, affordable, and increasingly viewed as desirable by many political, corporate, and civic leaders. Widespread activities to reduce emissions of GHGs demonstrate that despite the partisan wrangling in Washington, ordinary citizens can begin addressing climate change now. The challenge will be for federal "leaders" to catch up.

TEMPERATURES RISING

Although Swedish scientist Svante Arrhenius first suggested in 1896 that CO_2 emitted from the burning of fossil fuel would lead to global warming, the issue did not receive sustained political attention until the 1980s. In 1992, the United Nations

Framework Convention on Climate Change set a goal of stabilizing atmospheric concentrations of GHGs at a level that would prevent dangerous interference with the climate system. In 1997, the world's nations gathered in Kyoto, Japan, to negotiate how to accomplish this goal. The resulting agreement—the Kyoto Protocol—has now been signed by 100 nations and, if ratified by Russia, will go into effect later in 2003.

The protocol, which would require the United States to reduce its GHG emissions to a level that is 7 percent below 1990 levels, met a frosty reception in Washington. One senator pronounced it "dead on arrival." During his presidential campaign, George W. Bush pledged to reduce CO_2 emissions, but shortly after taking office reneged on this pledge. All rhetoric aside, it will be nearly impossible to stabilize global CO_2 concentrations without the full and active cooperation of the United States. U.S. citizens are 4 percent of the world's people but produce 25 percent of all GHGs. U.S. emissions are larger than the combined emissions of 150 less developed countries. Texas alone produces more CO_2 than the combined emissions of 100 countries, and the utility American Electric Power produces more than Turkey.

Several developments are driving the ground swell in climate action programs. For one thing, scientific understanding of climate change has advanced significantly. In 1992, the National Academy of Sciences cautiously concluded, "Increases in atmospheric GHG concentrations probably will be followed by increases in average atmospheric temperatures." By 2001, the academy was much more definitive: "Greenhouse gases are accumulating in Earth's atmosphere as a result of human activities, causing surface air temperatures to rise. Temperatures are, in fact, rising. . . . There is general agreement that the observed warming is real and particularly strong within the past 20 years."

Reports issued by the Intergovernmental Panel on Climate Change [IPCC], an interdisciplinary group of more than 2,000 scientists, show a similar evolution. In 1990, the panel stated that the "unequivocal detection of the enhanced greenhouse effect from observations is not likely for a decade or more." In 1995, it said that "the balance of evidence suggests a discernible human influence on global climate." In 2001, the panel concluded that "there is new and stronger evidence that most of the warming observed over the last 50 years is a attributable to human activities."

Another factor fueling the growth of climate action programs is that climate change is becoming evident, even to lay people. New England gardeners notice that spring arrives about two weeks earlier than it used to, Inuit hunters confirm the rapid melting of Arctic sea ice, and rangers in Glacier National Park document rapidly vanishing ice fields. According to the National Oceanic and Atmospheric Administration, the 10 warmest years in the historical record have occurred since 1980; 1998 was the warmest year and 2002 was the second warmest. It has now been 17 years since the world has experienced a cooler-than-normal month. This sort of unending heat wave has not gone unnoticed.

The human role in climate change is no longer a controversial theory to be debated on talk radio; increasingly, the public views it as a fact. And surveys show that people are concerned. For example, a recent poll revealed that 75 percent of registered voters (including 65 percent of Republican voters) believe that doing nothing about global warming is "irresponsible and shortsighted." The business community's perception of climate change also has changed. In the face of the accumulating body of scientific evidence, denying the problem is no longer a credible corporate strategy. Many powerful corporations that once lobbied against climate action have performed an about-face. Ford, for example, recently ran an ad that read: "Global Warming. There, we said it." In public policy as in corporate affairs, once a problem is acknowledged, the discussion turns to possible solutions. It is against this evolving scientific and political backdrop that politicians, corporate executives, and citizens are beginning to act.

STATES LEAD THE CHARGE

Many states are large emitters of GHGs. For example, 30 states emit more CO_2 than Denmark, 10 states emit more than the

Netherlands, and Texas and California together emit more than all the nations of Africa combined. Efforts by states to reduce their emissions thus have global ramifications. And states have important regulatory power over many activities that are relevant to the issue of GHGs.

Some of the most significant activity has occurred in California. In 2001, the legislature passed an $800 million energy conservation bill aimed at reducing the state's electricity use by 10 percent. Although primarily intended to address the state's electricity crisis, the law also will lead to strong reductions in GHG emissions. In 2002, the legislature took aim at motor vehicles, which account for 40 percent of the state's CO_2 emissions, directing the California Air Resources Board to develop a plan for the "maximum feasible reduction" in CO_2 emissions. Since burning a gallon of gasoline produces 20 pounds of CO_2, the obvious way to reduce emissions is to improve fuel efficiency. Today, a typical car produces nearly 12,000 pounds of CO_2 each year—roughly one pound per mile driven. Sport utility vehicles and light trucks pollute more. Noting that federal fuel efficiency standards have barely budged in two decades, California's governor, Gray Davis, said, "I would prefer to have Washington take the lead, but in the absence of that we have no choice but to do our part." The auto industry has objected that the proposed changes, to take effect in 2009, cannot be accomplished and would not be acceptable to consumers. (Automakers raised similar objections to previous fuel economy targets, emissions limits, seatbelts, and other advances). However, because 10 percent of cars sold in the United States are purchased in California, the state's law (if it survives legal challenges) may become a de facto national standard, since automakers are unlikely to build a separate line of cars solely for that market.

Electric utilities produce 38 percent of the nation's GHGs and are an obvious target for reductions. New Hampshire passed a precedent-setting bill that requires Public Service Company of New Hampshire, the state's largest utility, to reduce CO_2 emissions to 1990 levels by 2007. The bill was supported by a bipartisan coalition that included environmental groups and the utility itself. "We knew that there would be new legislation," said company spokesperson Martin Murray, "and we also knew that if we were involved in developing it, it would be more likely to emerge in a form we could support; collaboration achieves better results than fighting."

Oregon and Massachusetts also have passed laws requiring cuts in CO_2 emissions from power plants. A 1997 Oregon law required new power plants to emit 17 percent less CO_2 than existing ones. Developers can offset plant emissions by contributing to energy conservation efforts, developing renewable energy projects, planting trees, or using the plant's waste heat in nearby buildings. Generators that violate the standard are allowed to purchase credits from those who reduce emissions more than required. In Massachusetts, the six power plants in the state that produce the most CO_2 are now required to reduce their emissions by 10 percent by 2006–2008. Plants that fail to meet the deadline must purchase emissions credits.

New Jersey has committed to reduce GHG emissions by 2005 to a level that is 3.5 percent below 1990 levels. Under the state's comprehensive plan, one-third of the reductions will come from efficiency improvements in buildings, one-third from greater use of clean energy technologies, and one-third from improvements in transportation efficiency, waste management, and resource conservation. New York is providing $25 million in tax credits to building owners and tenants who increase energy efficiency. Maryland is waiving its sales tax on efficient refrigerators, room air conditioners, and clothes washers. In Oregon, appliances that are 25 percent more efficient than federal standards qualify for a tax credit.

States also are addressing climate change by promoting carbon-free renewable energy sources, such as wind and solar power. In 1999, George W. Bush, then governor of Texas, signed a bill requiring the state's electricity providers to develop 2,000 megawatts of renewable capacity by 2009—and this goal has already been achieved. Under this renewable portfolio standard (RPS), energy providers can develop the capacity themselves or purchase credits from solar, wind, hydro, biomass, and landfill gas projects. A surge in wind power development was spurred by the synergistic effect of the RPS and a federal tax credit for wind energy production. (The federal credit is set to expire at the end of 2003, unless extended by Congress.) Maine, California, Wisconsin, Arizona, Minnesota, Iowa, Connecticut, Nevada, New Jersey, New Mexico, Pennsylvania, and Massachusetts also have adopted RPSs. These programs will collectively produce enough carbon-free electricity to power 7.5 million homes, according to calculations by the Union of Concerned Scientists. This is the equivalent of taking 5.3 million cars off the road or planting 1.6 billion trees. The annual CO_2 savings equal about one-half of 1 percent of the nation's total emissions.

Some states are enhancing their impact by banding together to address climate change. Six New England governors joined premiers of eastern Canadian provinces in pledging to lower, by the year 2020, greenhouse emissions to a level that is 10 percent below 1990 levels. The pact calls for reducing electricity emissions by using more clean-burning natural gas, increasing renewable energy sources, and promoting energy efficiency. Signed in 2001 by three Republican governors, two Democrats, and an Independent, the pact demonstrates strong bipartisan support for curbing global warming. "This agreement sends a powerful message to the rest of the nation about the importance of working cooperatively to cut pollution," said Jeanne Shaheen, then the governor of New Hampshire. "If we're going to be successful, it means not just working on it in New Hampshire."

The attorneys general of seven states, New York, Massachusetts, Maine, New Jersey, Rhode Island, Washington, and Connecticut, recently notified the U.S. Environmental Protection Agency of their intent to sue the agency for failing to regulate CO_2 emissions under the federal Clear Air Act. The attorneys general of 11 states wrote to urge President Bush to cap power plant CO_2 emissions and increase automobile fuel efficiency. The chief legal officers of Massachusetts, Alaska,

Maine, New Hampshire, Rhode Island, Vermont, California, New York, Connecticut, New Jersey, and Maryland wrote, "Far from proposing solutions to the climate change problem, the administration has been adopting energy policies that would actually increase greenhouse gas emissions." The authors urged the president to "adopt a comprehensive policy that would protect both our citizens and our economy."

This coin has another side, however. A number of states, including Wyoming, West Virginia, Pennsylvania, North Dakota, Colorado, and Alabama, have passed resolutions barring state action to reduce GHG emissions or urging Congress to reject the Kyoto Protocol, or both. It is probably no coincidence that these states are among the nation's largest coal producers. In states where coal provides the bulk of the electricity, a family's $100 electric bill represents the mining of 1,400 pounds of coal, whose burning creates nearly 3,000 pounds of CO_2, most of which will still be in the atmosphere a century from now. But in a sign of the times, some of these same states are now developing climate action plans.

CITIES AT WORK

More than 100 cities already have pledged to cut their GHG emissions. For example, the San Francisco Board of Supervisors in early 2002 unanimously passed Mayor Willie Brown's bold resolution to cut the city's emissions over the next 10 years to a level that is 20 percent below 1990 levels (a 13 percent greater reduction than would have been required under the Kyoto Protocol). "When Washington isn't providing leadership, it's critical for local governments to step in," Brown said, adding that the goal "is as much about protecting our national security as it is about protecting our quality of life."

Since city governments own buildings, operate motor vehicle fleets, and regulate such things as utility rates, energy codes, mass transit, highway construction, outdoor lighting codes, waste management, land use, and other activities that have large climate effects, there are many policies they can adopt to reduce GHG emissions. A brief sampling of measures that have been incorporated into climate action plans includes the integration of transportation and land use policies in Portland, Oregon; altering the commuting behavior of municipal employees in Los Angeles; and purchasing hybrid electric vehicles for municipal fleets in Denver. Aspen, Colorado, now levies the world's highest carbon tax on profligate energy use in high-end homes, raising $1.9 million that has been used to install solar hot water systems, buy wind power, fund rebates for energy-efficient appliances, and retrofit public buildings.

The International Council for Local Environmental Initiatives offers guidance to cities through its Cities for Climate Protection campaign, in which municipalities commit to inventory their GHG emissions, set a target for future reductions, develop a local action plan, and verify its results. More than 500 cities worldwide (including 125 U.S. cities), representing 8 percent of global GHG emissions, are participating in the program. Cities have found dozens of ways to reduce or offset emissions, including tree planting, mass transit, renewable energy, lighting retrofits, mechanical upgrades of public buildings, installing light-emitting-diode bulbs in stoplights, stronger energy codes for new buildings, carpooling, and bike lanes.

Complementing public actions, individuals and private organizations are getting into the CO_2 reduction act. Students at the University of Colorado increased their student fees to purchase the entire output of a large wind turbine, thus saving 2,000 tons of CO_2. In Pennsylvania, 25 colleges are purchasing wind power. A religious group called Episcopal Power and Light is recruiting churches on the East Coast and in the San Francisco Bay area to buy wind energy. Families have an important role to play. The typical U.S. household produces more than 43,000 pounds of CO_2 per year, or 120 pounds per day. Half of these emissions come from heating, cooling, and operating the family home, while half come from driving cars. Not only are many families cutting back on use of fossil fuels, they are taking other steps as well. The federal Office of Energy Efficiency and Renewable Energy estimates that nationwide about 400,000 households are buying carbon-free electricity from their utility companies. In Colorado, 26,000 families and hundreds of businesses are participating in a "green pricing" program that has helped fund two \$30-million wind farms. This program, which has counterparts in many states, keeps 180,000 tons of CO_2 out of the air each year. By spending \$5 per month on wind power, a Colorado family can save 4,800 pounds of CO_2 each year—an 11 percent reduction in its climate impact for less than 20 cents per day. Driving a more efficient car, weatherizing their home, and installing compact fluorescent lights in place of incandescents can double these savings.

CORPORATE CLOUT

A growing list of prominent corporations, including automakers, oil companies, and electric utilities, have voluntarily committed to reducing their GHG emissions. By their public pronouncements, these corporations seem to have concluded that climate change can no longer be ignored and that responsible companies must engage the problem. Among Fortune 500 companies, there is an increasing belief that it is only a matter of time before GHGs are regulated, so beginning now to reduce emissions and factor climate change into long-range planning is a smart strategy. Some corporations have concluded that climate action presents an attractive business opportunity. For others, including electric utilities, the uncertainties of future climate policy cast a huge shadow over investment decisions, including whether to build new coal plants or retrofit aging ones. This risk of uncertainty, of not knowing what federal regulators may ultimately require, has begun to seem more financially hazardous than does resolving the matter.

The notion that cutting CO_2 emissions will devastate the U.S. economy is not borne out by experience. As manufacturers evaluate their energy use, they are discovering that many reductions are profitable and thus enhance their competitive position. For example, IBM reduced its total energy use by almost 7 percent in 2001, saving \$22.6 million and 220,100 tons of CO_2 emissions. Corporations also are discovering that they can increase productivity while simultaneously reducing emissions, further challenging the belief that economic growth and CO_2 reductions are incompatible. DuPont has reduced its GHG emissions to 63 percent below 1990 levels (primarily by reducing nitrous oxide emissions and other byproducts of fluorocarbon manufacture) and has held energy consumption flat since 1990, despite a 36 percent increase in company output. The company views its climate change activities as a way to prepare "for the market place of 20 to 50 years from now—which will demand less emissions and a markedly smaller 'environmental footprint' from human activity."

Among other corporate actions, Alcoa has pledged to reduce GHG emissions by the year 2010 to a level that is 25 percent less than 1990 levels. Dow has committed to reduce energy use per pound of product by 20 percent. In 1997, BP was the first major oil company to declare that action to reduce climate change was justified. The company, which supplies approximately 3 percent of the world's oil, pledged a 10 percent reduction in its own emissions (not those produced by the fuels it sells), and reached that goal in 2002, eight years ahead of target. By using less fuel to produce its products and by burning off ("flaring") less natural gas at oil wells, the company saved an estimated $650 million. According to the company's chief executive, John Browne: "People expect successful companies to take on challenges, to apply skills and technology and to give them better choices. Well, we are ready to do our part—to reinvent the energy business, to stabilize our emissions—and, in doing so, to make a contribution to the challenge facing the world." BP is betting that, in the long term, its solar subsidiary will profit from exponential growth in photovoltaics, a market that is doubling every three years. The idea that climate change represents a new business opportunity also is taking hold among automakers. The commercial success of hybrid electric cars from Toyota and Honda has pushed Ford, Daimler-Chrysler, and General Motors to announce that this fuel-saving option will soon be available in their vehicles.

Nongovernmental organizations are helping corporations address the climate challenge. The Pew Center on Global Climate Change (with 38 companies on its Business Environmental Leadership Council) and Environmental Defense's Partnership for Climate Action help corporations identify cost-effective strategies for reducing their GHG emissions. Participating companies share lessons they have learned in order to piggyback on each other's success. Most companies begin by reducing their lighting loads and upgrading their factories' heating, cooling, and pumping equipment. Some of the resulting savings are then often spent to buy clean power, further reducing emissions. Prominent companies buying wind energy include Kinko's, Lowe's Home Warehouse, Advanced Micro Devices, Patagonia, and Toyota.

THE ROAD AHEAD

A skeptic might fairly point out that CO_2 emissions in the United States are still rising, and that by 2010 emissions are likely to be about 25 percent higher than they were in 1990. Two important reasons for this rise are immigration and lifestyle choices. The nation has added more than 30 million people and 25 million motor vehicles since 1990, roughly equivalent to grafting on another California. At the same time, consumers are using 10 percent more energy per capita than two decades ago as people drive more and choose larger homes and automobiles. A typical U.S. citizen now produces about a million pounds of CO_2 in his or her lifetime.

Against this picture, is it really possible to forge at the grass-roots level a climate action plan that will be sufficient to the challenge? Probably not. To achieve the goal of stabilizing GHG concentrations in the atmosphere, emissions will need to eventually fall to nearly zero. It is difficult to see how this can occur without federal action. In this light, the news is mixed. Most of the federal government seems at loggerheads over issues related to global warming, and the Bush administration remains firm in its opposition to the Kyoto Protocol. However, a number of federal agencies are quietly conducting voluntary programs to reduce CO_2 emissions. In addition, Sen. John McCain (R-Ariz.) and Sen. Joseph Lieberman (D-Conn.) recently introduced a bill to cap CO_2 emissions and launch a market for economy-wide trading in them. This type of system has been successful in reducing sulfur dioxide emissions. The cap would be adjusted over time as needed to achieve climate goals, and large polluters would be required to purchase emission allowances in a CO_2 marketplace. It also has been suggested that the federal government should place a tax on CO_2 emissions. With either a cap-and-trade system or a tax, putting CO_2 into the atmosphere would no longer be free, something economists say is critical to addressing the climate challenge in an economically efficient manner.

States may play an important catalytic role in promoting national action. "If several large states, such as California, New York, and Pennsylvania, were all to pass similar legislation, it might be possible to actually begin to develop a national carbon emissions trading regime before any formal action is taken at the federal level," according to Granger Morgan of Carnegie Mellon University. This is roughly how the trading of nitrogen oxides among the states of the Northeast developed. But unlike with nitrogen oxides, states would not have to be located next to each other for CO_2 trading to make sense, because CO_2 mixes globally, and a ton saved anywhere has value anywhere else.

Given the clear need for a national solution, are states and cities in danger of overreaching as they begin to regulate emissions? Again, probably not. Congress recently rejected proposals to adopt a national RPS and to set stricter federal automotive fuel efficiency standards. Therefore, states are doing the right thing to push the debate on these issues. In addition, these programs provide a laboratory for learning what approaches work best, so that as the programs expand, eventually to the national level, there will be a variety of lessons to draw on in structuring the most workable and cost-effective strategy.

People working to reduce emissions around the country recognize that state efforts are no panacea, and they would eagerly applaud a more active federal role. As the group of attorneys general wrote to President Bush in 2002: "State-by-state action is not our preferred option. . . . It may increase the uncertainty facing the business community, thus potentially making the most cost-effective solutions more difficult." They also pointed to a recent Department of Energy report that concluded that the United States "could address carbon dioxide emissions issues with minimal disruption of energy supply and at modest cost, but only with fully integrated planning. Such integrated planning would be best promoted by the regulatory certainty that would result from comprehensive regulatory action at the national level." Such statements illustrate that by failing to provide leadership, the federal government is instigating a proliferation of varying state standards, on everything from cars to utility regulation, that will be more difficult for businesses and more expensive for consumers.

An economy-wide cap-and-trade system or CO_2 tax would result in wide-ranging market-driven changes that would supplant the need for the many other federal emissions reduction programs. But short of such a comprehensive strategy, there is still a great deal that Washington could and should be doing. The Bush administration currently favors a voluntary approach that recognizes corporations that offer to meet certain reduction goals. But the scale of the climate challenge ordains that a voluntary approach will not suffice. To gradually but thoroughly reengineer the nation's energy systems to be free of CO_2 emissions, new energy technologies will be required. R&D [research and development] is urgently needed for advanced vehicles, less expensive and more efficient photovoltaic cells, advanced biofuels, a hydrogen infrastructure, methods to capture and sequester carbon dioxide, and other vital technologies.

Providing a great deal more federal funding for the development of tomorrow's clean energy technologies is thus crucial. Maintaining or expanding federal support for today's renewable energy resources, such as the production tax credit for wind power, is also imperative. Federal economic encouragement will have synergistic effects with state programs as well, in getting new technologies into the marketplace and increasing their volume enough for economies of scale to drive down their costs. In addition, setting more aggressive federal efficiency standards for energy-consuming equipment from air conditioners to automobiles would help (as opposed to the recent rollback of air conditioner standards and the miniscule suggested increase in fuel economy for automobiles). And it is essential that Washington reengage in the evolving international response to climate change.

To say that Washington should do more does not mean that the surging tide of subfederal activities is not moving the political debate. These activities are demonstrating that there is a political appetite for carbon reductions, that such reductions are often profitable (though as reductions proceed, their cost is expected to rise but still be affordable), and that many climate initiatives have numerous economic and environmental benefits. The Bush administration rejects mandatory GHG reductions on the grounds that they would harm the nation's economy, yet many states taking climate action are doing so partly because it benefits their economies and leads to greater energy independence. Improving energy efficiency that improves the bottom line and developing renewable energy sources that reduce costs, pollution, and dependence on foreign oil are just the kinds of steps that the federal government could be taking to address both economic and security concerns at the national level.

Thus, many U.S. citizens are, indeed, taking responsibility for climate change—and are demonstrating in countless ways their willingness to invest in solutions. Although the scale of the challenge is daunting, eliminating a billion tons of CO_2 begins with the first ton. Each of the activities at the grassroots level reduces emissions, provides lessons about how to reduce them further, and perhaps most important, brings pressure to bear on the federal government to initiate the comprehensive strategy that is urgently needed. How long will it take for Washington to feel the heat?

Asato, Cathy. "Beneath the Surface." *Blue Planet.* Fall 2002.

Connelly, Joel. "Frontal Assault." *National Wildlife Federation.* August 2004. Available online at *http://www.nwf.org/.*

Dunn, Seth. *Reading the Weathervane: Climate Change from Rio to Johannesburg.* World Watch Institute Paper #160. Available online at *http://www.worldwatch.org/pubs/paper/160/.*

Glennon, Robert. "The Perils of Groundwater Pumping." *Issues in Science and Technology.* Fall 2002. Available online at *http://www.issues.org/issues/19.1/glennon.htm.*

Hassol, Susan Joy, and Randy Udall. "A Change of Climate." *Issues in Science and Technology.* Spring 2003. Available online at *http://www.issues.org/issues/19.3/hassol.htm.*

Helvarg, David. "Undiscovered Country." *On Earth.* Natural Resources Defense Council. Spring 2002. Available online at *http://www.nrdc.org/onearth/02spr/ocean1.asp.*

Postel, Sandra, and Brian Richter. *Rivers for Life.* Washington, D.C.: Island Press, 2003.

Sachs, Jessica Snyder. "The Greatest Show on Earth." *National Wildlife Federation.* February/March 2003. Available online at *http://www.nwf.org/.*

Shanks, Bernard. "The Heart of the Nation." *This Land Is Your Land.* San Francisco: Sierra Club Books, 1984, pp. 3–15.

U.S. Environmental Protection Agency. *Air Quality Planning and Standards: The Plain English Guide to the Clean Air Act.* Available online at *http://www.epa.gov/.*

———. *Clean Air Rules 2004.* Available online at *http://www.epa.gov/.*

———. *Introduction to the Clean Air Act.* Available online at *http://www.epa.gov/.*

FURTHER READING

Dowie, Mark. *Losing Ground: American Environmentalism at the Close of the Twentieth Century.* Cambridge, MA: MIT Press, 1995.

Glennon, Robert. *Water Follies.* Washington, D.C.: Island Press, 2002.

Postel, Sandra, and Brian Richter. *Rivers for Life.* Washington, D.C.: Island Press, 2003.

Shanks, Bernard. *This Land Is Your Land.* San Francisco: Sierra Club Books, 1984.

Turco, Richard P. *Earth Under Siege: From Air Pollution to Global Change.* New York: Oxford University Press, 2002.

WEBSITES

Issues in Science and Technology
http://www.issues.org/

National Wildlife Federation
http://www.nwf.org/

Natural Resources Defense Council
http://www.nrdc.org/

U.S. Environmental Protection Agency
http://www.epa.gov/

World Watch Institute
http://www.worldwatch.org/

INDEX

INDEX

INDEX

YAEL CALHOUN is a graduate of Brown University and received her M.A. in Education and her M.S. in Natural Resources Science. Years of work as an environmental planner have provided her with much experience in environmental issues at the local, state, and federal levels. Currently she is writing books, teaching college, and living with her family at the foot of the Rocky Mountains in Utah.

Since 2001, DAVID SEIDEMAN has served as editor-in-chief of *Audubon* magazine, where he has worked as an editor since 1996. He has also covered the environment on staff as a reporter and editor for *Time, The New Republic*, and *National Wildlife*. He is the author of a prize-winning book, *Showdown at Opal Creek*, about the spotted owl conflict in the Northwest.